REBELS OF THE NORTH

How Land Policy caused the Civil War

BY
GRANT DINEHART LANGDON

ISBN-13: 978-0-9790860-1-4

Table of Contents

Foreword

I REMEMBER MY FIRST TRIP TO COPAKE FALLS IN OUR OLD YELLOW truck. Dad sent Homer, one of our men, to pick up some supplies for our farm. I was old enough to ride along. Copake Falls was bristling with energy. One of the four express trains from New York had just unloaded. All three stores were busy. Some of the families of Mount Washington, who came down the steep rugged mountain roads that twisted their way past Bash Bish Falls, were there to pick up their mail and shop. Homer pointed out the old Taconic Inn where Babe Ruth would stop to have a drink or two when he came up to go hunting on the mountain. There was a ball field next door where people from the surrounding communities would gather and watch young men play baseball on Saturday night.

True, the iron works had shut down by then, but if you go back to Colonial times, Copake Falls, New York and Mount Washington, Massachusetts were on the knife's edge of change. It was back in the 1750s that the families on both sides of what is now the border were intertwined in an American revolution; it was for land ownership. Here, the old Colonial land policy of New York was being challenged. Much is written about land reform in China, Ireland, South America, and even Russia. Little had been written about the American Land reform that started here in Colonial times.

The first white settlers in New York were the Dutch. The English took over from the Dutch in 1664, but the boundaries between Massachusetts and New York were uncertain. The Dutch had claimed all the land east to the Connecticut River. The British King granted the Boston Bay Colony all the land west to the Hudson River. The conflict to the south was settled first with the establishment of the Connecticut border with New York. Further north the boarder conflict between New York and New Hampshire was settled after the American Revolution. That disputed land was admitted to the Union as the State of Vermont.

The conflict over the border between the Boston Bay Colony and Colonial New York placed the farmers of Mount Washington and Copake in conflict with the rich landlords of New York. The clash started when Massachusetts surveyed new townships and started issuing titles to land that Livingston had already rented to tenants.

It is impossible to grow up in Columbia County without hearing the names of Livingston, Van Buren, Van Rensselaer, and Samuel Tilden. These people were not only giants in Columbia County but in the nation, just as the nation started growing west. They all played a part in the dispute. I am a descendant of some of the rebelling tenants that stood up and started the protest. It became known as the Anti-Rent War, but it was not a protest over high rent, but a rebellion by farmers demanding ownership of the land they cleared, settled, and worked.

Just as in Europe, these tenant farmers paid rent and worked the land of the manor. However the American landlords had paid little for the land but had all the rights that the British Nobility enjoyed with their manors. The Anti-Rent War demanded an end to this feudal land system. That system was cemented in place by the well-connected Robert Livingston after the English took over in New York. Colonial land policy granted huge landholdings to these well-connected people that rented it to thousands of tenants. The huge land holding of Van Rensselaer, gained under Dutch rule, was granted standing as a manor under the English law. Like on the English manors, the owners lived in grand manor houses but the farming was done by tenant farmers. Because the tenants owned no land, they had no right to vote. They were bound to the Lord of the Manor by the feudal leases that required a day's work each year as part of the rent. When a tenant died the rights and obligations of the lease passed to the eldest son. The Lord of the Manor had his own judges and had his own militia to protect the interest of the Crown. The Lord of the Manor demanded all the tenants pay their rent on rent day at the manor office. Under British law, the eldest son had the right to inherit everything. That kept the manor intact and included the title of Lord of the Manor.

The clash over land ownership in Colonial America started in the 1750s between the Lords of the manors on one side and the Puritan settlers of western Massachusetts and the tenant farmers on the other. The Puritans that settled in Massachusetts came to America for religious reasons. The Cavaliers of Virginia came for profit. As Massachusetts settled west they gave 100 acres to new settlers for free; that gave them the right to vote. When the tenants of the manors saw this they demanded change. They too demanded ownership of the land and the right to vote. These rebellious farmers along the Massachusetts–New York border influenced land policy for the nation. That was because, as their population grew, the sons moved west and settle small farms. As the southern population grew, the Cavaliers of the South, who ran the politics down there, wanted slavery to create a new market for their growing slave population. They wanted larger farms and plantations. They demanded that the first Northwest Land Ordnance, written by Thomas Jefferson, be changed to permit slavery south of the Ohio River. That change in land policy set the stage for our Civil War.

The Civil War was not fought to preserve the Union, or to end slavery. It was fought to settle land policy for the western land. The southern plantation owners had their vision of a west with slavery. They were successful in preventing the passage of a Homestead Act. Lincoln was born in the slave state of Kentucky. His father, a small farmer, could not compete with the slave owning plantations. Lincoln had his vision of the West; it was small farms and didn't allow slavery. When the South left the Union Lincoln passed the Homestead Act of 1862, which was supported by the North. It gave free land to new settlers. It was a major plank in his platform that got him elected.

Babe Ruth and Zek Whitbeck
Photo courtesy of Betsy Garrett

Robert Livingston and His Family

WHEN THE FIRST EUROPEANS CAME TO AMERICA THEY BROUGHT A new concept of land ownership with them. The Indians had no concept of individual ownership of land and believed you could only own what you cultivated and occupied. The European concept was that the king owned all land and disposed of it as he pleased by granting title to an individual and that, later, could be inherited. Pennsylvania was granted to William Penn to settle an old debt. You didn't have to cultivate and occupy the land to own it. Charles II was king when the British took over New York. He gave it to his brother, the Duke of York. Later the Duke of York would become King James II after Charles II died.

Livingston knew how to work the system. He was 33 in 1687 when he got two King's Grants totaling about 400 acres of "good land" plus 2,200 acres of woodland. His first grant was made in 1684, and he described it as 200 acres of good land and 1,800 of woodland. In June of 1685 he petitioned for more land. He said his first grant was of "very little being fit to be improved." He then described a flat of about 200 or 300 acres and said "it might in time provide a convenient settlement for your humble servant." He reported the Indians called the place "Tachkanick." He was granted a license on June 3, 1685 and told the patent had to be taken out by the last day of September. He purchased it from the Indians and had the Indians go around to point out the boundaries. After he had it surveyed, the estate turned out to be more than 160,000 acres. The Indians had somehow been persuaded to be quite generous in pointing out the boundaries. He also was given manorial rights for his grant and became Lord of the Manor. As Lord of the Manor he was responsible for administration of the laws within the manor with two Courts-leet and a Court-baron. A Court-leet was a judge that dealt with criminal matters and the Court-baron a judge that dealt with misdemeanors and punished offenses committed by tenants. As Lord of the Manor he maintained his own militia. It was his duty to defend his grant and the people living there and come to the aid of the Kingdom. Livingston paid an annual quit rent of 20 shillings for the first grant and 8 shillings for the Taconic grant. It took 20 shillings to make a pound. As Secretary of Indian Affairs he received 100 pounds a year. In 1705 he also received the Westenhook patent from Lord Cornbury that extended his manor to the Housatonic River.

Livingston's life was in constant conflict. Back in England, King Charles I was executed in 1649, and Cromwell took over. In 1660 after the English Civil war, the Monarchy was restored and Charles II, from Scotland, became king. Charles II died in 1685 and his brother, the Duke of York, became King James II. James's first wife was Protestant and they had two daughters, Mary and Anne. James's second wife was Catholic and they had a son in 1688. Religion split the country. The Glorious Revolution of 1688 overthrew James II to prevent his Catholic son from ascending to the Throne of England. Parliament made William of Orange and Mary, his wife, king and queen. James II was forced to flee to France where he died in 1701. In New York, Jacob Leisler, a German, led the insurrection against King James in 1689 and was in control. Livingston, being from Scotland, was a strong supporter of the direct Stewart line of James II. He was known as a "Jacobite" and was forced to withdraw from the providence. The New York revolt ended two years later when Leisler was executed. When things quieted down Livingston was restored to his posts. By this time, he had also picked up the jobs of collector of excise and quit rent, clerk of peace, and clerk of the Court of Common Pleas at Albany.

He took a trip back to England in 1695 and made friends with a shipmaster, William Kidd. Kidd, like Livingston, was the son of a Scottish minister. Livingston was so impressed with him that he talked to the Earl of Bellomont, the Royal Governor, and they helped get him licensed as a privateer against the French and pirates. Livingston called Kidd a "bold and honest Man." The Earl could get the license, Livingston could get the money, and Kidd was the strong swashbuckling kind with the ability to run the ship, do the fighting, and bring home the cash. They signed the agreement on October 10th. They were counting on a tidy profit. One half of the profit would go to the king, and Livingston and Bellomont would split the rest. They outfitted Captain Kidd with a ship, the *Adventure*. It had 30 guns and 155 men. Captain Kidd's adventure against the French had problems, and they went off on their own and were not particular as to whose ship got plundered. He set sail for the Red Sea area and the Madagascar area of the Indian Ocean looking for pirates. Food ran short and there was an outbreak of cholera that killed one third of the crew. At one point, there was a mutiny, and Kidd killed one of his gunners. They

captured several small Moorish vessels and had a battle with a
Portuguese warship. One of his richer prizes was the *Quedagh Merchant*, an Armenian ship. This caused the East India Company to
complain to London. In 1698 the *Adventure* grew leaky, and the
booty was transferred to a captured sloop. The *Adventure* was sunk
off Madagascar, and Kidd returned to Oyster Bay, Long Island. He
buried his treasure on Gardiners Island. The Gardiner family had
been granted manorial rights and owned the entire island. The
Lord of the Gardiner Manor was told that if anyone touched the
treasure it would cost him his life. Kidd was probably looking for
Livingston and Bellomont for protection at that point. Captain
Kidd later set sail and was captured off Boston and returned to
London where he was tried and hanged for the murder of his sea-
man in 1701. His body was left hanging on the scaffolding for a
week as an example to others and to quiet the public outcry for
what he did. Kidd, though, had maintained he was innocent of
piracy to the end and was never convicted on that charge according to one source. The Crown sent a party with the map that dug up
and recovered the treasure about three years later. The Gardiner
family still has the receipt the Crown gave the Lord of Gardiner
Manor for the treasure. Queen Anne used at least some of the
money to convert the unused Royal Palace at Greenwich near
London to a hospital and retirement home for old seamen of the
Royal Navy. No doubt this too helped quiet the outcry of what
Kidd did. Parts of the Royal Seamen's Home is open to the public
today. The chapel has a magnificent painted ceiling. I have little
doubt that if the Crown got its share then Livingston got his share.

Because of Livingston's involvement with Kidd and the lack of
accounting for the government funds he handled as collector, he
had trouble after Bellomont's death in 1701. He was stripped of
his offices and had to return to England. This time his ship was

captured by a French privateer. He was given rough treatment and eventually he was put ashore. Back home he kept performing the duties of his offices even without pay. In 1705 he got a warrant from Queen Anne restoring all his offices and collected his back pay. It seems likely to me that the recovery of Captain Kidd's treasure from Gardiners Island played a part, and perhaps Livingston was the one that had the map.

The Colonial Assembly was still smarting from the missing funds. They were determined to recoup at least some of the funds, so they retaliated by abolishing the salary for Livingston's positions. Livingston continued to perform the duties of the office. In 1709 Livingston ran for the Assembly from Albany, was elected, and got his salary reinstated again and collected his back pay. In 1710 he got lucky again and sold 6,000 acres to Queen Anne for the use of the German Palatines. They had been mercenaries and wanted protection from the French. The Palatines immigration was the largest mass immigration to the colony up to that time and amounted to 10% of the population of the colony. The colony was still mostly Dutch, and they felt uneasy about such a large foreign influence. The Palatines were to produce naval stores for the Crown. Livingston got the contract to supply them with flour and beer to be paid by the Crown. Apparently many died in these hard times, but Livingston apparently billed the Crown for the number of people who landed in New York and not the number he fed, as Lord Clarendon complained in 1710.

One of the orphans was sold as a printer's apprentice in 1710. He was John Peter Zenger. Zenger established a newspaper in New York, *the New York Weekly Journal* in 1733. When he printed something unfavorable to the Royal Governor, Zenger was arrested for libel, and the common hangman was ordered to burn his paper. The trial was held in Philadelphia. At that time, if you wrote something unfavorable about the government it was a crime even if it was true. Nothing could be written if it brought the government into disrepute. When Zenger won, it was a first step in establishing freedom of the press. The press had a right to print the truth even if it was unfavorable to the government. His acquittal in 1735 and how it affected British freedom of the press was a sign that America was coming of age. Important things were happening here and our freedoms were slowly taking hold.

Livingston's government positions, his land, and his contracts with the Crown made him a wealthy and influential man. His involvement with Captain Kidd and Queen Anne's recovery of the treasure probably played a big role. The agreement was he was to get one quarter of the profits. He was able to secure representation for the Manor in the Colonial Assembly in 1716. He took his seat as the Manor's Assemblyman and then became speaker in 1718 and gained even more power.

Livingston Moves to Settle His Manor

MATTHUES ABRAHAM VAN DEUSEN BUILT HIS HOUSE UNDER THE lease given in 1687 by Livingston for 40 "morgans" of land, or about 85 acres, on "the Great Flatt." Matthues came from near Claverack on the Van Rensselaer Manor where his father leased a farm. His father and family lived close enough and, no doubt, came and helped at critical times like when Matthues had the timbers ready to raise for the house. Under Matthues's lease, Livingston supplied 8 milk cows, 2 mares, 2 geldings, 6 head of sheep, 1 sow, 200 fruit trees, and a strong young Negro of 14 or 15 for the cost of clothing, at Livingston's risk. The lease went on to describe the dividing of the increase in the livestock of which the landlord got one third, and were at Matthues's risk. It also described how the house, which was 25 feet by 22.5 feet, and barn, which was 30 feet by 60 feet, was to be built. Matthues had to clear and plant the 85 acres during the 10 years of his lease, but for his own profit. He was obliged to put 63 acres under the plow. He had to plant and prune an orchard of 200 trees, which

Livingston furnished, and build fences around the entire farm.
The last year he had to plant winter wheat. He had to pay rent
annually. The rent was 6 pounds of butter from each cow, two
brace of hens, and a yearling pig to be delivered in Albany in
October. At this time paper money wasn't in use and coins were
scarce so barter was important. It also gave Livingston goods to
use in trade. The lease also required 26 days work of two "servants"
on the road to the manor. It meant Matthues and the 15-year-old
slave. Matthues was paid for part of his work on the road, but one
day was considered his feudal duty. The lease ran for 10 years and
ended May 1, 1697. The lease was in the Roosevelt library in
Hyde Park, New York when Ruth Piwonka did her research.
Given the work involved in clearing the land, building the house,
building the barn, other improvements, the rent, and the increase
number of livestock, of which Livingston got one third and was a
major factor, this one 85 acre lease gave Livingston a yearly profit
on the entire 160,000 acres he purchased. Livingston's lease was
much harsher than the leases offered earlier by the Dutch West
India Company. They furnished each tenant with the same four
cows and four horses, some sheep and pigs, but the lease ran for
6 years and the company did not take a third of the increase. The
tenant only had to return the original number of animals.

The house Matthues built is just west of the village of Copake.
It's a friendly old house with floors that run down as much as a
foot in some rooms. There are lots of steps between rooms with
each room built on a different level. The walls are all crooked and
the floors creak when you walked. It is the oldest house in the
village. It was built by a brook on the edge of a clearing in the
wilderness when only the Indians lived close by. Robert Livingston, who received his grant to the land in 1686, called this place
the "Great Flatt at Taghkunic." Later it would be called the

Copake Flats, and then just Copake. The oldest part of the house is what we used for the dining room, kitchen, and a den when I was growing up. My childhood thoughts go back to the warmth of the wood stove in that kitchen. After getting wet and cold riding downhill in the snow we would all have some hot chocolate and bring our chairs up close to the stove. There were usually six or seven of us. We had fun around that stove, and it was a great place to be.

That part of the house is of stick and wattle construction. A strong frame was built of upright post and beams. Here oak had been split into sticks three or four inches square, and the ends were sharpened and were just long enough to fit into grooves cut in the upright posts. Then a mix of mud and straw was used to plaster on both sides of the sticks to make a solid wall. It was then whitewashed and covered with white muslin and another coat of whitewash. Later someone had covered the muslin with wainscoting on the inside and clapboards on the outside. The house was built in 1687. The only nails, which were furnished by Livingston, were used to hold the rafters at the top and were pounded out one by one by a blacksmith. An ax was the main tool used in constructing the house. The skill of the ax man was evident in the sticks we took from one of the walls during renovations. Each cut, made more than 300 years before, was precise, and each stick fit exactly in its groove.

Back then, the house consisted of two large rooms running north and south. The chimney was built over the east room near the center of the house. Three large beams ran north and south in this room, which we used as a dining room. The beams are of yellow pine and had hew marks in them until about 1920 when my grandfather had them taken out with a hand plane. He told me he liked smooth beams. The hand-wrought hooks once used to hang guns on the beams are still there. The beam to the west was made much larger than the others because it had to carry the weight of the chimney that was constructed from that beam up through a small garret. This was common in Dutch houses of the time. When my grandfather was a boy the garret was used as a place for the hired help to sleep. They would sometimes awake in the morning and find snow blown in on their blankets. Back when the house was first built, it was sleeping quarters for the slave, owned by Livingston and bound to the farm.

This east room, where the family lived, had the fireplace for heat and cooking, with a bed-sink to the south of the fireplace that extended to the south wall. During the day, a curtain would be pulled across to hid the bedding. There were several windows and doors to the north and south. To go from that room to the other part of the house you had to go out on the porch that extended across the front, to the south, and go through another door on the other end. Originally that part of the house may have been used to store grain and such before the barn was built.

It was in the east room that Matthues Van Deusen and his family lived. That part had a cellar, used for storage, entered from outside on the east. Later the fireplace was removed and that space used for a door to the other part of the house, which was our kitchen. A two story addition had been made about 1810. It was of post and beam construction and was more finished. It had two fireplaces and added four more rooms. In about 1920 a large dormer replaced the garret over the big rooms in the old part of the house. Many other smaller changes were made over the years. The first I can remember as a youth was the filling in of the hand-dug well directly in front of the door to the west room. In my grandfather's time there had been a large "summer kitchen" built near this area. That was to keep the heat from cooking out of the house. My grandfather was born in this house in 1889.

Copake and the Early Settlers

I ENJOYED WALKING ACROSS MY FARM. I LIKED TO WALK UP ON MY hill because of the view, and I liked to look at the crops here. The soil is the best on my farm; it's a deep limestone loam and, despite the hilly lay of the land, is some of the richest soil in the county. The corn here is always the best on the farm. The only problem here is you have to alternate corn with stripes of alfalfa to control erosion. I purchased the farm from the family in 1963 after I graduated from Iowa State University. The farm was 380 acres, and I was milking 130 cows.

It was late in the afternoon as I looked east from the hill. The sun was sinking low in the west behind me, giving a special brilliance to the things I saw. The reds were redder and the greens, greener. Everything was a little brighter and a little sharper that time of day. The little village of Copake was just under the hill. The white clapboard and Greek columns of the Methodist Church seemed to gleam. Across the farms in the valley lay Alander Mountain to the south, and Washburn Mountain with the Bash Bish gorge to the north. Bash Bish Brook threaded its way from Massachusetts through the rugged narrow gorge of the Taconic State Park, down past the village, and crossed the corner of my farm just under the hill. It passed from my sight just to my right. This is the most beautiful spot on the farm. All of the crops and the golden grain in the valley made me think of the song "America the Beautiful" with its Purple Mountains Majesty. It made me feel patriotic. It made me feel good to be alive that warm summer day.

As I stood there, I could not keep my mind from slipping back in time and thinking of the history of this insignificant spot. I thought of the people who settled here, raised large families, and how the sons and daughters moved west and changed America. If the Taconic Hills was in the cradle of democracy, it was also the nursery for the men that settled the West.

John Langdon settled here just after the French and Indian War. John grew up on Quaker Hill in Dutchess County on his father's farm. According to family tradition, three brothers came over from England to Boston. One brother settled in Connecticut where he became a poet. One brother settled in New York and became a farmer. The other brother settled in New Hampshire where he became a merchant. Later, John of the New Hampshire branch, fought at the Battle of Bennington and served as Governor of New Hampshire. He was one of the signers of the Constitution. His house is now a museum in Portsmouth, New Hampshire. The John Langdon that settled in Copake was a farmer. He had been stationed at Fort Stanwix, at Rome, New York during the French and Indian War. If you go to Rome, New York you can see the reconstructed fort near the center of town. John would later serve as a lieutenant in the Revolution. He rented one of Livingston's farms about one mile north from where I was standing. His farm had been worked before but the crops were never very good. He worked the soil deep and tilled it well. He first plowed his fields with a yoke of oxen and three horses hooked to a single plow. Neighbors were amused by his hard work, but he earned a reputation of being a good farmer when his crops were harvested.

On this farm, he raised a family of fourteen children. All the children of the first generation stayed in the area. One of his sons, David, purchased the farm from the Livingstons in 1826, but most of the later generations moved west. The Erie Canal opened in 1825 and offered a way to market crops from the cheap western land.

In 1760, Cornelius Vosburgh settled on a farm he bought about a mile and a half north of my farm. He had a family of four sons and four daughters. The first generation stayed in the area. Time has lost track of many of the children, but one son, Cornelius, Jr., married twice and had fifteen children. Three of the children died, three stayed in the area, and the rest settled in various parts of the West. This was typical of the early settlers. Descendants of these early settlers were the first to move to western New York, then down the Ohio River to Kentucky and Ohio, and then by lake steamer to places like Wisconsin and all the West.

William Dinehart was a young man who grew up near Heidelberg, in Baden, Germany. He went to Hamburg in May of 1753 and was invited by a Dutch sea captain to take an excursion with four other young men: Peter Rhoda, Peter Swart, Abraham Decker, and Jacob Haner. They were looking for a good time, and the Captain said they were only going out in the port a little and then come back. The Captain gave them a grand feast and had music and dancing along with strong drink to while away the time. The next morning, Whit Sunday, they awoke to find that the ship was not going back to port but was bound for New York. They had been shanghaied. It was a long passage with other stops, and the ship did not get to New York until fall.

When they got to New York they didn't have the seven pounds passage each the Captain demanded, so they were sold as indentured servants at auction, their indenture being long enough to pay the Captain his seven pounds. Lord Robert Livingston Jr. purchased them, and they were indentured for four and a half years of service. All five were taken to Ancram to work in the iron works. After their time was up, they were offered leases to farms on the manor. For the four and a half years they received only the shelter, food, and clothing that Livingston provided. William Dinehart accepted Mr. Livingston's "generous" lease and settled west of the outlet of Copake Lake, to the north of where I stood. He raised a family of ten children. The others accepted Mr. Livingston's offer too.

Twenty some years later, a muscular, blond German fur buyer came by the Dinehart Farm. It was a chance to earn a little extra money, and they were immediate friends. The youth was John Jacob Astor who also came from Baden, Germany. He was in his early twenties. He liked to visit and share news with William about Heidelburg and Baden, such as the destruction of Heidelburg Castle, which was struck by lightning and burned after William Dinehart left Baden. It was 1787, and he was buying fur that he would later take to London to sell.

Astor was born in Waldorf, Germany, the son of a butcher, and had spent four years in London with his brother, who manufactured musical instruments. When he came to America he was 21 and brought some of the instruments with him to sell. He arrived in New York in the spring of 1784. The first job he took was delivering baked goods around the city for a baker. After he learned his way around the city he took a job with Robert Bowne, an elderly fur trader. He worked hard, and it wasn't long before Bowne gave him more responsibilities. Bowne sent him as an agent on trips buying fur in the wilderness of New York State. It was rugged work, tramping through the wood alone with a heavy pack of furs on his back. On his own time he invested his money from his occasional musical instrument sale in furs brought in by Indians and travelers on the river. By late fall, when the river froze, he had enough furs to make it worth his while to travel to London to sell them.

The profit was huge, ranging from 600% to 1,000%. He had the advantage of already knowing his way around London, and now he got to know the fur buyers in London. Later he would do more business with them. He purchased more musical instruments and things to trade with the Indians. When he returned to New York he acted as an agent for Bowne on several expeditions and bought furs for himself in between. By the time he was 24, he only worked for himself. He established the American Fur Trading Company, and the business not only spanned the country, but his ships were the first to circle the globe. His ships did a lot of trade in the Orient. He purchased his fur mostly in the West and Canada, using agents. By 1820, he was the richest man in the country. When he sold the business, he invested the money in what was then farmland on Manhattan Island. Years later his family would be linked to the Dineharts when his grandson, Henry, married Malvina Dinehart.

The Dineharts purchased a farm a half mile west of where I was around 1810. Charity Ann, a daughter, was born to Elizabeth Snyder Dinehart and John Dinehart on this farm in 1834. At that time, the Indians were still living on the flat just to my north. It was their practice to migrate to Virginia in the fall to spend the winter and return in the spring. Elizabeth placed Charity Ann in a cradle on the porch one warm October day in 1834 and went about her housework. When she came out to check on the baby, Charity was gone. After talking with a neighbor who saw the Indians start their migration, they decided the Indians had kidnapped Charity. Twenty-three-year-old John quickly gathered together about twenty neighbors, and they rode after the Indians. Charity was recovered some fifteen miles away near Pine Plans. Feelings ran high against the Indians, and they never returned. Andrew Jackson, our fiery frontier general, was president, and Martin Van Buren of Kinderhook, twenty miles to the north, was his vice president. The two men worked closely together. Jackson, whose father was a tenant farmer, favored making Indian land in Georgia available to young settlers. He got the Indian Relocation Act passed by Congress about this time. Although the Indians of Taconic lived peaceably in the past, there is little doubt that John and his neighbors supported Jackson's and Van Buren's Indian relocation. The relocation took place mostly during the Van Buren presidency and was called the Trail of Tears. Many Indians died on the way to the Indian Territory.

The Sweets ran the hotel in town and had various farms. Originally they came from Devonshire, England in 1630. John Sweet was a younger son of Robert Sweet. When Robert died, John's older brother, Adrian, inherited the family estate called Traine in Moldbury under the inheritance laws at the time. John, his wife, and his three children came to Boston on the ship *Mary and John* with John Winthrop's fleet. They later went with Roger William to Rhode Island for religious reasons. Members of the family later moved to Dutchess County, and then Rowland Sweet came to Copake around 1800. The Holsapples were Dutch and also came over early. They too ran the hotel and had a farm to the west of where I stood, at Chrysler Pond.

In 1835, Lot Cook purchased 400 acres east of where I was standing. His father, Simeon Cook, as a young man had originally moved to Amenia, New York, about 25 miles to the south. He and his young bride had to cut their way through the wilderness from Hartford, Connecticut. He was a captain in the Colonial Militia. When the news came that the British regulars had fired on the Colonial Militia at the Battle of Lexington, everyone gathered in the square to hear the stories of what happened. Ephraim Pain, Esq., stood up and gave a moving speech in favor of independence. Then Captain Cook stood up and assembled his men. He addressed his men by saying, "Fellow soldiers, now is the time to give up our liberties, or defend them with the musket..." All of his men chose to follow him.

When the British Regulars fired on the Colonial Militia, General Gage had created a "we against them" situation. With that happening across the colonies, the new nation had an instant army of about 10,000 militia, and the Revolution began. General Gage at Boston had about 4,000 men. Simeon fought in the Revolution for seven years along with his three oldest sons, Mordicia, Nathaniel, and Simeon. Another son, Solomon, became a colonel in the war of 1812. Simeon was made a major and returned three times to raise more forces for important battles of the Revolution.

His wife, whose maiden name was Dunham, had come through the wilderness with him. She ran their public house at the center of the village while he was gone. She also ran their slaughterhouse and had a contract to supply meat to the Tory prisoners that were held in a stockade a half mile to the east of Amenia. The Revolution was more than a war for Independence; it was a war to determine who would be able to stay and who would have to go. It was a bitter war between neighbors. The militia that fought the war had nothing but the promise of land. They were fighting for a new life. The aristocrats that ran the war made the promise to help hold Washington's army together. The Revolution was good business for the Cooks. They got to stay and managed to purchase seven farms. The Tories went to Canada.

The Cooks had nine children in all, and Lot was the youngest. He was playing with some Tory children one day and came home and said, "Hooray for King George and all his royal family." According to some old family letters, he wasn't able to sit down for several days. He never said that again. He later married and had nine children, Alonzo being the youngest. Alonzo sold the farm and moved to Ancram to the south of Copake. Again many of the Cooks moved west.

The Revolution changed things but as this generation moved west they left the dominating evils of the feudal manor system behind. Hallenbeck, Loomes, and Reese, or Race as it was later known, all had farms near where I was standing. They were the real rebels that fought for land reform. When the Erie Canal opened in 1825, new opportunities opened up to the younger generation. It had always been possible to move west and settle, but now the canal offered a way to get the crops to market. A barrel of flour could be shipped from Buffalo for a fraction of the cost of the land transportation cost that was available before. The younger generation saw the opportunity to escape the grip of the landlords. The western land now became more valuable and the younger Dineharts were among the first in Taconic to move west. They included 17 grandsons that went to Monroe, Yates, Oswego, Steuben, and Tioga counties in New York, and then to Elkhart, Indiana; Ionia, Michigan; and into South Dakota, Minnesota, and California. When the western lands opened up, bread got cheaper in New York City. It was the independent farmer that grew the grain. It added to commerce and helped the city grow that only added to the demand. America was on the move.

The Foundation of the Land Reform Rebellion

I LOVED THE OLD STORIES I GREW UP HEARING. I LOVED TO READ THE history of this place. As I read the old documents and letters, a story unfolded to me. It was a story about the strong-willed Scot, Robert Livingston, setting up his feudal manor, like the ones in his native Scotland. It was about how land reform came to the manor. Livingston founded one of Colonial America's great fortunes and aristocratic families. Their income came from rent. This family alone went on to acquire more land and controlled more than a million acres at one point. This powerful family did much to shape the nation and win its independence. But, it was the rebellious settlers here that defied the Livingston and the laws of that time. They challenged the laws that kept the land in the hands of the aristocrats. The small farmers eventually won. They changed the Constitution of the state and helped define how the West would be settled.

Lord Robert Livingston I became Speaker of the Colonial Assembly in 1718, but then resigned as the Manor's Assemblyman in favor of his son Philip in 1721. Robert Livingston died in 1728.

Philip, the eldest son of the five living children, inherited most of the manor and Lordship of the Manor, giving him a place on the King's Council. Philip's main interest was as a merchant. He didn't live in the manor house his father built in 1699 at the mouth of the Roeliff Jansen Kill, but chose to live in New York City and Albany. In New York he not only had a store but also owned ships and was using family members and friends as agents to carry on trade in places like Boston, the Caribbean, and London. He saw a market for iron and established his own iron works on the manor in Ancram about 1743. Philip's son, Robert Jr., took his seat in the Assembly in 1737, and he inherited the manor and title after Philip died in 1748. He was now Lord of the Manor, Robert Livingston.

The thing that made land reform unique to this area was the boundary dispute between Massachusetts and the powerful land-holding Livingston and Van Rensselaer families of New York. Their use of tenant farmers on the scale of the Hudson Valley is unique in the United States. These families were among the richest and most powerful families in Colonial America. These families owned most of the land in this part of New York and ran it for themselves under feudal leases. It was a system that can't be called Dutch, or English, or French, because all the colonies, including the French in the St. Lawrence Valley, used similar laws. They all required a day of labor and allegiance to the landlord. They were simply feudal. Of the English colonies, New York was unique because it had powerful large estates. The owners bought over the feudalistic English Manor system with tenants to work the land. The South also had feudal laws that favored the aristocracy. With high value crops like tobacco, indigo, rice, and cotton, the Carolinas and the like used the more available slaves instead of leases with tenants.

Georgia was set up as a colony that prohibited slavery by James Oglethorpe in 1733. Things did not go well. In order to save the Colony the trustees allowed slaves to be brought in beginning in 1749. They simply couldn't attract enough tenants with the leases they were giving. Slavery brought on the growth of plantations in the South.

I stood high on the hill on my farm and looked at the low Taconic Mountains and the Berkshire Mountains beyond. The Taconic Mountains start at the New York border and extend to the Housatonic River that passes through Great Barrington and Sheffield, Massachusetts. From where I stood, the Massachusetts border was a scant three miles away across the valley. On top of the mountains is the town of Mount Washington, with the town of Sheffield and the Housatonic River on the other side. The settlers of these Massachusetts towns played a big part in what happened here.

The Massachusetts Bay Colony claimed land extending west to the Hudson River. The Dutch, of what was to become New York, claimed their land extended east to the Connecticut River. When the English took over New York from the Dutch, the colony held to the Dutch land claim. Lord Robert Livingston claimed his manor extended to the Housatonic at Sheffield and Great Barrington because of the 1705 land grant from Lord Cornbury. Fifty miles of wilderness, and a big part of Livingston Manor, hung in the balance. It was the struggle to settle this dispute that awakened the servant farmers that rented the land, like the Van Deusens, to demand ownership of the small farms they had cleared and worked. They demanded to own the land they worked, just like the settlers of Massachusetts.

The settlers of Massachusetts were different from the settlers of the other colonies, and that difference influenced how America developed. The difference can be accounted for by English history. James I was king from 1603 to 1625. He married the daughter of King Henry IV of France who was a strong Catholic. She was a strong influence on James and influenced how the Church of England was run. A group made up of farmers, merchants, professional men, and scholars went to James and asked him to purify the church of certain new ceremonies derived from the Roman Catholic Church. James's reply was, "I will make them conform or I will harry them out of the land." A band of puritans went to Holland in 1608, but after living there for a time decided to move on. They finally decided to go to America, but realized they needed backing. They sent a council back to England, and they were granted a license by the king to go to land run by the Virginia Company. They were joined by a group from England and landed in Plymouth, Massachusetts in 1620. They landed north of Virginia, their intended destination, but decided to stay there and forgo the help of the Virginia Company. They set up their own government to work out the differences between the English and the Dutch groups of settlers, and the Plymouth Colony was founded. In 1629 another settlement was made by John Endicott at Salem and given a charter as The Massachusetts Bay Colony. After King James I died, King Charles I carried out the "harry them out of the land" threat and thousands came to Boston from 1630 to 1640. In twenty years, Boston had gone from nothing to a city of 10,000. When the English Revolution took place the movement ended. It ended with the thud of the executor's ax on Charles's neck. Cromwell and his Protestants came into power and the church issue went away. The Protestants were called "round heads" because they wore their hair short and lived simply whereas the overthrown Cavaliers had long hair and lived lavish lives.

This group of farmers, merchants, professional men, and scholars that settled in Massachusetts also had a different view of land ownership than the settlers to the south in Virginia and the Carolinas. Settlers to the south were the Cavalier younger sons of the ruling class in England that supported Charles I. This group continued to go to the new land to escape the reach of Cromwell and his "round heads." They were bent on setting up an estate like their older brother had inherited back home and living the good life they had lived growing up. As the population of the Bay Colony grew, the pressure to settle new land increased. The Church, protection from the Indians, and social organization were important to these early settlers. When the New Englanders set up a new town, a common pasture was set up, and each family was given a deep strip of land of 100 acres free. The house was built in the village for protection from the Indians. It was a radically different way to develop the country than the plantation system or from Livingston's 160,000-acre grant with tenants paying rent and doing the work of developing his estate for him. Livingston's tenants could not vote. The yeoman of Massachusetts could vote. If conflict was to develop on land ownership it had to happen here! The Taconic Hills is where the two worlds collided in the 1750s.

As I read the old books, what unfolded was how the yeoman of Massachusetts settled west until they came in conflict with this powerful family. Here, under the Taconic Mountains, Massachusetts laid out three townships, five miles west from the mountains and seven miles north and south. On May 16, 1755, 110 men went out from Sheffield to lay out the three townships. It was reported they passed south along the foot of the mountains about a mile east of where I was standing. They camped out in the area and then moved north. The job wasn't done until May 24th when they returned to Sheffield. This defiant act by the New Englanders tempted the tenants of the Lords of the Manors looking for a way out of their feudal bindings. David Ingersoll was from Sheffield and had been meeting with the tenants and building support for the move. It fueled the conflict over land reform that didn't end until a century later.

The early families shaped land reform here. They demanded an end to feudal privileges of the aristocracy. As the trouble developed, some of the Van Deusens and others fled east to the safety of the mountain to escape the feudal demands of Livingston. They simply refused to pay rent for their small farms. Others took up the struggles against feudalism. The early settlers were the ones that fought French domination of the continent, and then British domination, in the fight for independence. Their sons and daughters were still rebellious and were fighting for ownership of the farms they settled.

Feudal Law at the Time of the Revolution

THE FIRST HINT OF REFORM FROM OUR FEUDAL PAST WAS THE American Revolution. By the time of the Revolution, English rule was well established. The Dutch turned New York over to Britain in 1664. The British defeated the French at Quebec in 1759 to settle the French and Indian war. The treaty settling the seven year war with France was signed in 1763. That ended France's claim in North America and India and ended the fighting in Europe.

English laws, like the laws of feudal France, were slanted towards the large land owners. Feudalism tended to produce extraordinary wealth for some and extraordinary poverty for others. Feudalism developed when the strong central government collapsed at the end of the Roman Empire about the year 500 AD. In some ways it was like the government of the Roman Empire. In the early days of the Roman Republic small farms existed. The farmers joined the army for a term of 14 years and went away to war. When they won a battle they sent the prisoners home as slaves.

The landowners who stayed at home used the slaves to take over and work more land, creating large estates for themselves. When the farmers came home from their 14 years of service they found their farms gone, and they had to move to the city. That was when Rome grew to a city of over a million people. The Romans compensated for poverty created in the cities by the development of the dole that maintained order. The slaves of Rome were allowed to gain their freedom under some circumstances, but near the end of the empire slave uprisings were not unheard of. A large uprising in Sicily lasted several years.

When order broke down from the fall of Rome, feudalism developed. Allegiances developed for protection as a series of wars between rival towns and invading Vikings and the like occurred. The end result was that a noble leader offered protection for surrounding farmers. He took title to the farmer's land in return for building a strong castle and the pledge to protect his farmers, maintain roads, act as a court to settle disputes, and maintain order. Usually the lord would not put the farmer off his land without good reason. If the farmer sold his rights, the landlord could claim a portion of the sale. If the farmer died, the lease passed to his oldest son. In exchange for his services, the landlord received work and rent, usually in the form of goods, from the tenant. The lord in turn might owe allegiance to another noble and paid a fee and provided services.

In Britain, the House of Lords was made up of the eldest sons of the old Lords that ruled the country. The highest title is Duke, then Marquis, Earl, Viscount, and Baron. By law, the oldest son inherits all: the land, the rent, the title, and the right to sit in the House of Lords. That kept the large estates intact and gave a small number of landowners control over the budget and the taxes. They voted their own interest and kept their own taxes low. That no doubt was one of the causes of the tax problem with the colonies.

The younger sons usually took up a profession, went into the army, or immigrated to places like America. Things remained pretty much that way in Britain until about 1910 when the popular Prime Minister, Lloyd George, was successful in reforming Parliament. In the BBC documentary *Born to Rule,* it was estimated that in 1910 only 10,000 people owned all the land in Britain.

Lloyd George submitted a budget in 1910 calling for placing taxes on the huge estates to finance his programs in health and so forth. Because of the 8% inheritance tax he proposed, the House of Lords refused to pass his budget for two years.

The House of Lords was eventually forced to give in, and there was a reform taking away much of their power. The reform extended to the House of Commons. Industrial cities like Manchester grew in population during the industrial revolution but their representation in the House of Commons stayed the same. Some small villages lost population and even disappeared but they had the same representation in the House of Commons as Manchester.

Had it not been for the American Revolution and the changing of the laws of inheritance so younger sons could inherit, American land ownership could have continued on the same as in Britain. If you look at South America with its huge plantations, some with thousands of people, you get an idea of what America could have been like if the laws did not change. In countries like Argentina that have lots of good land you have the very rich and the very poor. Even much of Ireland's problems can be traced to the British land policy in the 1800s. In Ireland the landlord put their tenant off the farms for their own profit. The landowners were mostly Protestant.

In America everything didn't change over night with the Revolution. The Federalist, Robert R. Livingston, with the help of John Jay, a family member, wrote the first Constitution of New York State. It required a person to be male and own 100 acres of

land debt free to be able to vote. This left the political power in
the hands of people like the Livingstons, Van Rensselaers, and
Schuylers. While the cry of no taxation without representation
echoed in the streets of Boston during the Revolution, most
people of the manor couldn't vote after the Revolution. It wasn't
just New York. The United States Constitution became law
March 4, 1789 and provides for the election of the president by
Electors. It provides that "each state shall appoint, in such manner
as the legislature thereof may direct, a number of Electors." There
was no popular vote for president until 1800. It was very much in
tune with the political thinking of the time. John Locke, the English Philosopher whose writings inspired the Declaration of Independence, drew up South Carolina's colonial constitution. Locke's
constitution was based on feudal principals and also encouraged
the aristocrats. South Carolina's Constitution, like New York's
Constitution, placed the power of the ballet firmly in the hand of
the rich. The tenant farmer had no say. The aristocrats of South
Carolina couldn't operate their plantations without slave labor.
When they consistently voted their interest it would trouble the
nation for generations. The aristocrats of South Carolina dogged
the nation to hold on to slavery with threats of secession for years
to come.

Even in the more democratic state of Massachusetts there were
problems. The wealthy merchants controlled the politics there.
When the economy turned bad they insisted on hard money to
protect the value of the wealth they had accumulated. That hurt
the farmers and lead to Shays's Rebellion in 1786.

American patriots like Sam Adams and James Otis from
Massachusetts had pressed for more rights for the people. The idea
wasn't popular with everyone though. Another event that changed
how people thought was the French Revolution that came in

1789. The bloody French Revolution caused people to be a little more democratic. To the ruling class, democracy wasn't welcome, but was better than having your head cut off in the guillotine, and little by little things changed. The Bill of Rights to our Constitution was enacted in 1791.

The French Revolution ended the feudal system in France and went further than the American Revolution. It, like the American Constitution, established that all men were born with equal rights, and guaranteed free speech. It was different because it gave all citizens the right to vote, and the amount of taxes you paid depended on your wealth. The long conflict between Britain and France was very costly, and taxes to pay for it were passed on to the common people by the landed nobility in both Britain and France.

The Revolution and the Sons of the Manor

When the American Revolution finally started, the Livingston family was leading the way. They didn't just have the manor, but they also had ships and stores, and they also engaged in trade. Perhaps the heavy tax load imposed on trade by the king and the House of Lords smarted. The original Molasses Act was passed in 1733 but was usually evaded by the colonial traders. It protected the British sugar plantations by creating a West Indian sugar monopoly. It was strengthened in 1764 and imposed a heavy tax. Livingston, like other American merchants, raised cash by trading American goods for molasses with the French and Spanish West Indies for resale. Now they could only deal with the British West Indies. Another problem with the merchants was tea. The East India Company was nearly bankrupt, and the king was forced to come to their rescue. A bill went through Parliament giving the company the right to ship tea directly to the colonies without paying the tax imposed on the American merchants. The tea would be sold through the company agents.

It cut the American merchants out of a profitable trade. Other problems existed. The people in Pennsylvania were dissatisfied with the sons of William Penn because they paid little taxes on their land whereas the common people paid the taxes imposed to pay for the French and Indian War as well as the rent. William Penn died in 1718, and his grand home, Pennsbury Manor, just north of Philadelphia, was left to decay. The sons preferred to live in London and didn't care what happened as long as the rent came in. Pennsylvania sent Benjamin Franklin to England in 1757 to get the Penns to pay their fair share of the taxes on their land and ease the burden on the common man.

Robert R. Livingston was a leading patriot in the family. The Dutch word for a stream is *kill* and is how the principal stream of the manor, the Roeliff Jansen Kill got its name. The first Lord of the Manor, Robert Livingston, built his manor house at the mouth of the Roeliff Jansen Kill in the early days. One night, the Indians were getting ready to attack the house and his second son, Philip's brother Robert, awakened the family and prevented a massacre. It was claimed that because of this Robert got special consideration. The 13,000-acre Claremont Estate, south of the Roeliff Jansen, was set off from the manor and was entailed to Robert. Robert wanted to call the estate Callendar for the estate of the Earl of Linlithgow in Scotland, the head of the family. Philip objected to his younger brother adopting such an imposing name for his smaller estate, and Robert settled on the name Clermont. Clermont is a city in France where other family members were living. He started an important branch of the family. His son was also named Robert, and he became an important judge on the King's Bench. He was influential and was an early supporter of Independence despite his connections with the Crown. His son, Robert R., was vital to the development of the country.

Philip's son, Robert Jr., was now Lord of the Manor. His iron works at Ancram produced part of the great chain placed on pontoons across the Hudson to prevent the British ships from coming up the river. Another son of Philip's, also named Philip, was a signer of the Declaration of Independence. The British plan to end the Revolution was to split the colonies by taking control of New York. The main objective of the British in New York was to advance up the Hudson and join up with Burgoyne at Saratoga. The fortifications at the chain anchors weren't strong enough, however, and in 1777 the British started the campaign by marching up along the riverbank and capturing the chain anchors. They released the chain from the east anchor and it floated to one side, letting their ships sail up river. First they burned Kingston and then went on to burn Clermont, Robert R. Livingston's manor house. The family received news of the advancement of the British and fled. Margaret Livingston hid the considerable 4,000-book library and buried the family silver. She oversaw the servants loading up all the belongings they could carry and left a nearly empty house. She could look back and see smoke coming from the house before they were out of sight. They were on the way to safety in Salisbury, Connecticut.

Robert R. Livingston was the most prominent member of the family. What made him a major target of the British was he was on the committee with John Adams, Thomas Jefferson, Benjamin Franklin, and Roger Sherman that prepared the Declaration of Independence. John Adams wanted to insure that Virginia would go in favor for the move for independence and selected Jefferson to draft the Declaration for that reason. The ideas in the Declaration of Independence were based on the essays of the English philosopher, John Locke. There is little reason to think the other members didn't contribute or approve. Livingston had originally argued against independence when the British occupied New York City. On July 9th the New York provincial congress voted to sign, and Philip Livingston signed for New York. Robert R. went on to bigger things. He served as Secretary of Foreign Affairs and later, as Chancellor of New York, he swore George Washington in as president. When Jefferson became president in 1801, he appointed the respected Robert R. Livingston to the important post of United States Minister to France. While he was in Paris, he became interested in Robert Fulton's experiments with the steamboat and became his partner. Fulton named his first steamboat after Livingston's estate, Clermont. It made its first run up the Hudson River in 1807 and stopped at the estate. Two weeks later it was put into regular service. Fulton eventually married into the family. In 1807, Fulton and Livingston built the first steamboat to go down the Ohio River at Pittsburgh that opened the western rivers to the steamboat.

Robert R. Livingston did the most for his country when he was Minister to France. He and some others convinced President Jefferson the country should purchase New Orleans from France to provide an outlet for goods down the Mississippi River. When Spain controlled the port of New Orleans, some western farmers even talked about quitting America to become part of the Spanish territory. Spain had gotten control of New Orleans from their French allies in 1762. The United States was able to get a treaty with Spain for access to the port in 1795. The problem developed again when Spain returned the Louisiana Territory to France in 1800. Jefferson didn't like the idea purchasing New Orleans because he, unlike the Federalist, didn't believe in a strong central government. Finally he went along and got approval from Congress to spend 10 million dollars for the project. He sent his friend, Monroe, to help negotiate the treaty. When Monroe arrived in Paris though he found Livingston had already agreed to purchase not just New Orleans but all of Louisiana for 15 million dollars. Livingston was hard of hearing but could speak French. He pointed out to Napoleon that the weak French navy would not be able to protect his western empire against the British fleet. Napoleon already had his Egyptian campaign ruined when the British under Lord Nelson destroyed the French fleet and prevented him from getting reinforcements. Now he didn't want to spend more money on a navy and was more interested in a land war in Europe anyway. He was also looking for allies and hoped that America would get involved with a war with Britain. Livingston pointed out that if America didn't get the port of New Orleans, American's interest was best served by siding with the British. The purchase doubled the size of the country. Andrew Jackson cemented the American claim to Louisiana at the Battle of New Orleans in 1815. The desk used in Paris to sign the Louisiana Purchase is the property of the Clermont Historic Site run by the State of New York as well as a fine portrait of President Jackson. When I visited Clermont, it moved me to see a relic that played such large part in shaping this country. The Jackson portrait was probably given to Robert R. Livingston's younger brother, Edward. He served as Secretary of State under Jackson. The Livingston family was one of the most important families to the development of America. Other present members of the family are former Representative Robert Livingston of Louisiana and former President George Bush's family.

Time was right for change, and change it did. What made the American Revolution such a big step forward in government was it wasn't against King George III, but it was against the entire system. It was the first big break from our feudal past. The Revolution ended the inherited power and wealth of the House of Lords in America. The second and third sons in America didn't like paying the taxes while their older brothers and cousins back in Britain inherited the family wealth, sat in the House of Lords, and passed the tax bills that kept their own taxes low. The new government forbid titles, and ended the right of the eldest son to inherit everything, including the political power. A new way of choosing political leaders had to be found.

When the Americans won the Revolution, the Tories that stayed loyal to the king lost their land. It was not just the large estates but many smaller ones too. The Revolution was America's first civil war. It pitted neighbor against neighbor and even brother against brother. The civil dissatisfaction wasn't just in America, but many in Britain were for the Americans. They had brothers, cousins, friends, or such living in America and were hurt by the same taxes. After the war, most of the Tories went to Canada or back to Britain. One Livingston family member was a Tory and was held under house arrest by the family on one of their estates on the Hudson. Had the Revolution gone the other way, you could imagine him becoming the new Lord of Livingston Manor. There is little doubt Robert R. would have gone to France. Perhaps the Livingstons could be in front because they had a back up plan. Whatever their thoughts, the Livingstons certainly served the nation well during the Revolution.

The manor system ended after the Revolution. Lord of the Manor, Robert's oldest son, Peter, was the heir apparent to the manor and lordship. In anticipation of his inheritance he began construction on a manor house worthy of the Livingston name. He named it the Hermitage, and it was planned on a grand scale with a 60-foot entry hall. It was only partly done when the Revolution broke out, and everything changed.

After the Americans won the Revolution, there would be no Court-leets and Court-barons and no private militia and no Lord of the Manor. The big change for Peter, though, was the change in the inheritance laws, the abolition of entail and primogeniture. Many of the early settlers were younger sons who came to America when the eldest son, back in England, inherited everything under English law. The second and third sons now had their say. All sons could inherit equally under the new American law. Because the Revolution upset trade, Peter had a reversal in his business in New York and now had to share the estate with his brothers. Construction had stopped during the Revolution. After the Revolution it was certain that it wouldn't be finished. He put the roof on the one floor that was finished. The Hermitage was finished on the original plan in the twentieth century only to be demolished by a later owner. The land east of the post road was divided between brothers Walter, Robert C., Henry, and John Livingston, who inherited the Copake area.

For the tenants of Livingston Manor everything had changed but everything remained the same. Under the first New York State Constitution you still had to own 100 acres free and clear to vote. There was a new government, but the rent and taxes still had to be paid, and the Livingston family still held the political power. The landowners voted their own interest. The Livingstons were still very much in control.

During the Revolution the soldiers were promised land for their service. When the Tory estates were taken over two years after the war, the land didn't go directly to the soldiers. It then took four years before the land office was set up and somehow the estates wound up in the hands of the politically powerful, like the Livingstons. The soldiers for the most part would have to wait until the passage of the Northwest Ordinance in 1787 or rent a farm from the aristocrats, like the Livingstons and Van Rensselaers.

The Northwest Ordinance

AFTER THE REVOLUTION, THE NATION HAD A PROBLEM TO SOLVE concerning its western land. Connecticut, Massachusetts, Virginia, Georgia, North Carolina, and New York had western land, and some of the claims overlapped. The land extended to the Mississippi River for the most part, and it wasn't entirely clear if Britain would honor the claims. The British still had troops in some areas. Maryland had no western land and argued that these states should cede the western land between the Appalachians and the Mississippi River to the central government. The states started ceding their land to the central government in 1781. The question then was what the government would do with the land. Thomas Jefferson of Virginia wrote the Ordinance of 1784 defining how the ceded territory would be developed. He called for ending slavery in the new territory and establishing ten new states. Some areas like Kentucky, which was part of the Virginia claim, already had some settlers and slaves. The last battle of the Revolution was fought at Blue Lick in what is now Kentucky.

The Ordinance of 1784 wasn't satisfactory to some of the states that still had not ceded their western land. They demanded it be changed. The plantation owners held the political power under the feudal laws of the time. They measured their wealth by the number of slaves they owned. A new market for slaves in the West would maintain their wealth. Jefferson's 1784 Ordinance was replaced by new ordinances as compromises were reached. One in 1785 set up how the western land would be surveyed and governed and finally by what became known as the Northwest Ordinance in 1787. The new ordinance only covered the land north of the Ohio River but still prohibited slavery. By superseding the old ordinance the land south of the Ohio River was left open for slavery. The ordinance defined how new states would be admitted but as the country extended west it would be half free and half slave. It was a victory for the aristocracy of the South that owned slaves, and they defined how the country would grow. The stage was set for the Civil War.

The Ordinance provided for the formation of between three and five new states. The land was to be laid out in townships six miles square with each town having 36 sections per mile square. Each section has 640 acres, and each town had one section set aside for schools. Land was sold in sections only, at a dollar per acre. Congress appointed a governor, a secretary, and three judges. The first governor was Arthur St. Clair. He made Merriet on the Ohio River his capital. The ordinance was more democratic than the New York State Constitution that required 100 acres free and clear to vote. The requirement in the new territories was only 50 acres. It provided that when the territory got 5,000 adult males who owned at least 50 acres, they could elect their own assembly and have a Legislative Council of five members. The Legislative Council was chosen by Congress from ten people recommended by the assemblies. It included a Bill of Rights and provided that when a territory had a population of 60,000 it could be admitted as a state. The state had equal rights of representation with the original states. The people who wrote it remembered when they were colonist they had less say about such things as taxes than their brothers living back in Britain did.

The 981-mile Ohio River runs from Pittsburgh past Louisville, Kentucky to the Mississippi at Cairo, Illinois. It was the highway to the west for the settlers. According to Henry Christman's book, *Tin Horns and Calico*, the first settlers to come in numbers were from New England where small farms were the rule. Connecticut had early claims to some of the land and reserved some land for its settlers, typically a group of about 10 people traveling together. They would have horses, cows, pigs, and sheep and have a covered wagon. The animals needed time to forage and the men needed time to hunt and fish. The trip from Connecticut to Ohio, about 600 miles, was said to take 90 days in 1805. Moving to western New York was a more reasonable destination.

Former President U.S. Grant was born at Point Pleasant, Ohio in 1822. His family was probably typical of the movement west. His father first moved to western Pennsylvania from Tolland, Connecticut. Then Grant's father, Jesse, left the Pennsylvania home and worked his way down the Ohio River moving and working from farm to farm as a young man. At Maysville, Kentucky he took a job in a tannery where he learned the trade. After he married he move down river to Point Pleasant to start his own tannery. The 27-year-old Jesse and his 22-year-old wife lived in a rented one-room cabin. The cabin is preserved as a museum and reflects some of the riggers of frontier life.

Matthues Van Deusen's move to the Taconic flat of about 15 miles had been compatibly easy. His first advantage was the short distance. His second advantage was he had an extra hand in the form of a slave to share the work. Many settlers moving west, south of the Ohio, would make the move easier by taking along slaves. Most settlers, especially in the North, had little capital and no slaves. To them, Indian corn became known as the poor man's capital. The early frontier settlers who survived had farming skills and were determined. The first thing they did if they arrived early enough in the spring was plant corn. Then, while the crop was growing, they built the house and tended the animals. In a few months, if things went well, they had food for their animals and their family. The cornhusks furnished their bed and the cob their fuel. That was their capital until the younger animals grew and the other crops came in. So many people died trying to move west that if a person died they were said to have "gone west." When the farms developed enough to have surplus corn, they used it to feed hogs that were first driven east over the mountains. An easier way to market the corn was to turn it into whisky and sell it in the east. After the Revolutionary War, veterans went west to receive their war bounty of land. General Ruffis Putman was their leader, and he made the first settlement at Marietta, Ohio. Connecticut had reserved some land for its settlers when it ceded its western territory. Life was hard on the frontier. The Indians were allied with the British and they raided the early settlers. It wasn't until 1794 when Anthony Wayne defeated Little Turtle at the Battle of Fallen Timbers near Toledo that it changed. That battle was of major importance because it not only set the boundary of the new territory and got the British to leave, but it cut down on the Indian raids. Even then the British didn't formally withdraw from the Northwest Territory until the Jay Treaty with Britain in 1796.

Settlers were still bothered by Indians, but this opened up the area. The result was a population of 250,000 people by 1810. The 1811 battle at Tippicanoe in Indiana brought about another treaty with the Indians. Land was made available in smaller plots by then, and as more Indians made peace, more people settled in the territories. Ohio was admitted as a state in 1803, Indiana was made a territory in 1800, and the government opened a land office there in 1807. Indiana was made a state in 1816. Michigan was made a territory in 1805, but public lands weren't opened to settlement until 1818. It was admitted as a state in 1837. Wisconsin was made a territory in 1836 and a state in 1848. Robert R. Livingston and Robert Fulton sent the first steamboat down the Ohio River in 1811, and by 1820 regular service started and the Ohio became a major route west.

Thanks to how the Northwest Ordinance was written, the aristocrats on their plantations held the advantage in the South. Kentucky, which was part of Virginia, was admitted as a state in 1792. Tennessee was admitted as a state in 1792. Mississippi was originally part of North Carolina. The government opened a land office there in 1807, and it was made a state in 1817. A land office was opened in 1809 in Alabama, and it was admitted as a state in 1819. The Spanish had traded Florida to the British in 1763 for Havana. Florida was loyal to Britain in the Revolution. Then the Spanish attacked west Florida and occupied it in 1779. British ceded Florida back to Spain in 1783, and then it was ceded to the United States in 1819. Florida was made a state in 1845.

One of the most important and colorful presidents of the United States was Andrew Jackson. He became popular because of winning the Battle of New Orleans in the War of 1812. The British had 10,000 troops and lost 2,237. Jackson had 5,500 and lost only 71. As president, he set the course America would follow for at least the next generation. Jackson's father was a Scot-Irish tenant farmer who came from Ireland. Andrew was born in the Carolinas. His father died just before he was born, so he grew up being poor. As a boy Jackson was rebellious and feisty. He fought in the Revolution and became a prisoner of war at the tender age of 14. When a British Army officer ordered him to polish his boots, Jackson refused in such a manner that the officer struck out with his sword. Jackson carried the scars for the rest of his life. Later he lived on his own in Charleston for about a year where he developed a love for fine clothes and had fine manners. Although he never had much schooling, he became a lawyer and moved to Tennessee. He was best known as the spokesman of the West and the common man. He fought several duels, killing one man, and people respected him not just for his determination, but also out of fear. You just didn't cross Andrew Jackson. Most people loved him because of his rugged straightforward frontier code. He carried a bullet from one of his duels to the end of his life.

Modern historians rank Jackson quite low. It is probably because he owned slaves and because of his relocation of the Indians. However, if Jackson isn't the man of the 21st century, he was certainly the man of his time. He was extremely popular with the common man. Jackson was our first president born in a log cabin, and it was easy for the poor farmers and tenants to relate to him. At his inauguration he threw the doors of the White House open to anyone who wanted to come, and the place was overwhelmed by a huge, rough crowd of common men that loved him. Jackson did several important things. One was that he expanded suffrage, giving more common people the right to vote. Other presidents followed him and claimed humble beginnings, and he made it easier for a man of the people like Lincoln to become president. Jackson used the spoils system to form the Democratic Party. He dismissed a lot of government workers and replaced them with his own loyal followers. He didn't trust the aristocrats who controlled politics and government, and he didn't care if they knew it. Jefferson thought he would be the ruination of the country; he was right. He ruined it for the governing elite. He was for western expansion and the common man. When he relocated the Indians, he opened up much of Georgia and the West to settlement. He won solid support for the Democratic Party from the small farmers that lasted for years.

Andrew Jackson, a Democrat, was popular with the common people. The small farmers of the North supported the Democratic Party because of Jackson until James Buchanan. Buchanan, from Pennsylvania, was a Democrat, but he vetoed the Homestead Act. The South threatened to leave the Union, and they didn't like the Homestead Act. Buchanan vetoed the Homestead Act to win favor with the planters. That veto cost the Democrats the small farmers' vote. The Homestead Act was a defining issue for the small farmers. The small farmers of the North wanted a Homestead Act and helped start the Republican Party. Lincoln took up the issue of the Homestead Act as a main plank in his platform. Lincoln won the election in a nation divided by the slavery issue.

Shays's Rebellion and Land Reform

An idea took root with the boundary skirmish in Taconic. That idea was that the settlers who cleared and worked the land had a stronger right to the land than Livingston. Robert Livingston Jr.'s grandfather paid little and used political influence and legal sleight of hand to gain control of his 160,000 acre manor. The farmers who cleared the land, set up the farms, and worked the soil saw themselves as equal to Livingston. New York was one of the most important founding colonies and influenced how the American West was settled. As the sons of the small farmers moved west they carried that idea and spirit of independence with them. They believed that if they did all the work of clearing and settling the land they had a right to the ownership. History books treat the Anti-Rent war as a minor movement along with the Whisky Rebellion and Shays's Rebellion, or they ignore it altogether.

Shays's Rebellion, however, came at a critical time in the nation. The new country was governed under the Articles of Confederation. In a way the Anti-Rent War was like Shays's Rebellion that took place across the Taconic Hills in Massachusetts. Shays's

Rebellion was the common farmer against the rule making aristo-crats and merchants of Boston. During the Revolution, the Continental Congress authorized a large amount of currency, or bills of credit, through the federally chartered banks where they deposited their gold and silver. Many people wouldn't accept what they saw as a worthless currency for trade. The different states also authorized state banks to issue different amounts of currency, or bills of credit, based on the deposits of gold and silver they had. For example, it took 6 Massachusetts shillings to equal a federal dollar, while it took 8 New York shillings to equal a dollar. The aristocrats and merchants of Boston wanted to keep the value of the paper currency high, so it could be redeemed for gold and silver needed in international trade. The Revolution had disrupted the Massachusetts economy. The debt before the Revolution was 100,000 pounds. After the war the debt was 1,300,000 pounds, with the soldiers due 250,000 pounds. Most of the tax to support the debt was collected by the poll tax. After the Revolution, the method of collecting taxes did not change. Business was also disrupted by the Revolution. Nantucket had 150 fishing boats before the Revolution and employed 2,500 men. After the Revolution they had only 19 boats. Normal trade was also cut off. Congress had already imposed a 5% import duty, and there was not enough money in circulation to pay private obligations, including the taxes. To please the merchants and still try to ease the shortage of gold and silver, the Massachusetts legislator passed the Tender Act of July 3, 1782. It had been legal to pay taxes with cattle back in the mid-1600s in Massachusetts because of the lack of gold and silver money. That is also why Robert Livingston collected his rent in butter, chickens, pigs, and so forth. Massachusetts now called for the payment of private debt with real estate and personal goods, such as cattle, again. The goods were to be appraised in court by an impartial party.

Farmers objected to the cost of having to go to court to do business because they were already going broke and being foreclosed on. The rebellion got its start after representatives of about 50 towns held a meeting at Hatfield where they discussed the problem. In August 1786, groups of protesters prevented the sessions first of the Northampton court, then in Great Barrington, Concord, and Worcester. Similar problems took place in New Hampshire. Shays confronted a state force of 600 at Springfield and prevented the court from meeting. In November of 1786 Job Shattuck was captured, and the rebellion was put down in the eastern part of the state. When Shays, with a force of 1,200 men, threatened to take over the federal arsenal at Springfield, General Benjamin Lincoln and the militia of 4,400 men defended the arsenal in December. Later, in February, Shays was defeated at Petersham.

Shays's Rebellion was one of the things that led to the adoption of the Constitution in 1788. Shays's Rebellion pointed to the need for the new Federal Constitution because when the Revolution was put down, the leaders fled to New York, Rode Island, Vermont, Pennsylvania, and so forth, and the state had been unable to deal with the problem. Also, the money problem had to be dealt with. Congress dealt with the money problem by establishing the Federal Mint in Philadelphia in October of 1786. The Constitution established a strong central government and gave more rights to the people. The leaders of Shays's Rebellion were all caught, condemned to death, but later pardoned. Shays later moved to New York State.

The anti-renters did not threaten a government arsenal or result in a new Constitution and the establishment of United States Mint, but Shays's Rebellion and the Anti-Rent War were still important. It was a movement that started before the American Revolution, and it lasted almost a hundred years. Shays's Rebellion lasted from August 1786 to February 1787. Second, it involved the idea of the ownership of land and was influential to the setting of land policy for the West. It was not just a group of farmers protesting high rent. They wanted ownership to the land they settled and more. In a poster announcing their meetings with Peter Finkle, the Columbia County leader, they called themselves "the Friends of Equal Rights." Like Daniel Shays, they wanted equal access to the government. They questioned the right of a privileged person like Livingston to run things just because of his political influence and inherited wealth. They questioned if Livingston's title to his 160,000 acres was legal. He only paid quit-rent, the tax to support schools, on a fraction of what he claimed. They wanted to own their farms, and they wanted to be their own masters and have say in the government.

The English had hardly set foot at Jamestown in 1607 when the Dutch started settling to the north, starting at what is now Albany on the Hudson River and then at Manhattan around 1611. By 1613 they had settlements on the Delaware River and by 1617, on the Connecticut River near Hartford. They claimed all the land between these rivers. In 1620 the Pilgrims landed at Plymouth and set up a colony. Then in 1628 the Puritans set up the Massachusetts Bay Colony, first at Salem and then at Boston. By 1640 Boston had a population of 10,000 people.

The English colonies to the east started settling west and didn't recognize the Dutch claims. In 1667 the Dutch were forced to turn their colonies over to the English. This created a conflict because the colony of New York now had an English charter that respected the old Dutch claim. The boundary for Connecticut was settled in 1705 at 20 miles east of the Hudson River. The boundaries between New York, Massachusetts, and New Hampshire were left in dispute. These colonies gave conflicting grants to settlers.

When the Livingstons and Van Rensselaers first claimed their land, forest spread out from the Hudson River in both directions. If you walked east from the river on an Indian trail, you would be under a canopy of trees that was only broken by three open spaces on Livingston's vast 160,000 acres. Van Rensselaer owned 700,000 acres, much just north of Livingston's land. If you kept going, things were much the same until you got to the Connecticut River. Small settlements were made there, first made by the Dutch and then the English of Massachusetts Bay Colony as they moved westward.

Just after Robert Jr., Philip's son, became Lord of the Manor in 1748, the settlers of the Massachusetts Bay Colony began to move west of the Taconic Hills. By this time, settlements were established in Stockbridge and Sheffield. As the first settlers moved west of the mountains, Livingston threatened them to get them to pay rent or drive them off. Then in December of 1751, Massachusetts Bay Colony sent in surveyors to lie out a large farm for Michael Hallenbeck and Josiah Loomis. This was too much for Livingston. If the Bay Colony was going to help his tenants claim his land he wanted New York to defend his claim. He petitioned the New York council to intervene against Massachusetts on his behalf. The council did what any council would do; they did nothing, but said he should seek a remedy in the courts.

In 1753, William Bull and 57 other settlers petitioned the Massachusetts Bay Colony for a land grant. The Stockbridge Indians, with a different concept of land ownership, sold it to William Bull. It covered an area ten miles by about six miles, and started at the big mountain west of Sheffield. It covered a good part of Livingston and Rensselaer Manors and included much of the Copake and Hillsdale area. When nothing happened to them, others were encouraged. Massachusetts eventually laid out three townships.

Each town was five miles west from the Taconic Mountains and seven miles long. The Massachusetts Bay Colony was offering a hundred acres of unimproved land for free, and was charging two shillings for each additional acre. Among the brave early settlers that took up the Massachusetts's offer was Robert Pain, one of Livingston's woodcutters, George Robinson, Nehemiah Hopkins, and the persistent Josiah Loomis.

The Conflict for Land Reform Begins

ROBERT LIVINGSTON JR. WENT ALL OUT TO PROTECT HIS INTERESTS and make full use of the courts. Pain was arrested by Livingston for cutting trees and was taken to Albany. When his friends from Massachusetts showed up with the usual 10 pounds bail provided by the Bay Colony, his bail was set at 1,000 pounds. Mr. Pain had to remain in jail. Robinson had his house burned by Livingston, and was arrested.

Loomis was an ore digger for Livingston at Ancram. He started farming, and had worked his farm for several years but refused to pay rent. Livingston at first had warned Josiah off, but he kept on farming, claiming where he farmed was part of Massachusetts. Livingston decided he had to be dealt with. He took sixty armed men and rode into the yards of both Robert and Johannis Van Deusen, Matthues Abraham Van Deusen's son and grandson. Both Robert and Johannis paid their rent and had farms on lease. They were bound by the lease to help Livingston. It was part of their feudal duty to the Lord of the Manor, and now he demanded his day's service to the manor. He took them along to harvest Loomis's crops. The wheat was hauled away in Loomis's wagons. Livingston ordered the corn crop destroyed and Loomis's possessions put out in the road.

Massachusetts's officials over in Sheffield weren't amused. They swore out warrants and the Van Duesens were arrested for trespassing and taken to the gallows in Massachusetts. Captain Ingersoll, a leader of the Massachusetts settlers from Sheffield, headed the group. Livingston later had to pay "thirty-odd pounds" damages and fourteen pounds court costs to secure their freedom. He also complained to the Governor of New York, who issued a proclamation for the arrest of the persons involved.

Massachusetts formed a local militia of about a hundred men to protect the settlers. Captains Robert Noble and John Hallenbeck headed it. Hallenbeck was a Dutchman who had also been one of Livingston's tenants. Plans were made to erect two forts in the area. Michael Hallenbeck, whose son John helped in the arrest of the Van Deusens, was taken prisoner by the Livingston forces and taken to the gallows in Dutchess County. The land south of the Roeliff Jansen Kill was part of Dutchess County. He was held without bail. There was an exchange of letters between Governor Clinton of New York and Governor Shirley of Massachusetts. Governor Shirley complained about the ill treatment of his citizen, Michael Hallenbeck, who wasn't even involved in the arrest. Clinton claimed there must have been a mix up about the bail issue and denied he was held in a dungeon or that one even existed. The matter ended without more embarrassment when Hallenbeck escaped.

By this time, the farmers were organized. They sent groups around to the various farms trying to get them to stop paying rent and urging them to give up their farms. Livingston was annoyed by the "banditry up in the mountains," where many had fled, who paid visits to his tenants but didn't pay his rent. This included Hendrick Brusie, Adam Shefer, and Jacobus Van Deusen.

Just to the north, Robert Noble and his militia arrested Sheriff Yates of Albany County. Yates was trying to serve a warrant for Van Rensselaer. Noble took him to Sheffield where he was bailed for 150 pounds to stand trial. The Governor of New York issued a proclamation for the arrest of Noble and the others who helped him.

John and Henry Van Rensselaer set out to end the matter. They worked closely with their cousin, Livingston, and with this proclamation and forty armed men, tried to arrest Noble at his fortified house. They only got four of the men he was after, one of which was Josiah Loomis. Noble had gone to Sheffield. Noble's wife was home and after they broke open a chest and took the guns and some desperate negotiations she promised to get her husband to pay rent. The Van Rensselaers took their men and left. After leaving Noble's house, they went to Nehamiah Hopkins. Hopkins wasn't home so they tore his house down. They set up camp nearby to get an early start the next day.

The Van Rensselaers and their posse had gotten up early and went to Livingston Manor. They were after William Reese. The raid came just at first light. Van Rensselaer watched as his men broke down the door. Reese was startled and desperately forced his way out through the garret roof. He was trying to escape when he was shot and killed. Reese's body had seven wounds. He was shot in the back with buckshot.

The officials in Massachusetts issued warrants for the murder of Reese. The Sheriff from Springfield took a force of more than a hundred and descended on Livingston's iron works at Ancram. They arrested several of the people who had been present at the murder of Reese. They were all employed by Livingston at the iron works where Livingston produced carriage wheels and shot for the French and Indian War that was in progress. The people arrested had been warned about the raid but went willingly. The Lords of the Manors had simply gone too far. The person who shot Reese, Matthew Furlong, was safe in custody in New York, so they were held as hostages for the release of the Massachusetts people.

Livingston complained he needed his men to produce the shot and wheels for an expedition against the French who had a fort at Crown Point to the north. The matter was more or less settled for the time because of the war. The French had sent the Indians on raids to the Kinderhook, Claverack, Stockbridge, and Sheffield areas. In Kinderhook, a raiding party carried off a young boy and a Negro, and a man named Gordonier was scalped He escaped in that condition and lived. Robert Livingston responded with his militia, but the Indians escaped and they saw no action. At Claverack, a woman and two children were carried off. Up at Hoosic, near the Vermont border, a more serious raid took place. Five hundred Indians burned the village and murdered many of the people.

To defend the manor against the people from Massachusetts, Livingston built his own fort with a hundred men and three swivel guns. He maintained an armed guard to protect himself against arrest. In May of 1757, Livingston and his men attacked the anti-renters in the fortified house of Jonathan Darbie. Several people were killed, and Livingston forced the rest to flee east to Sheffield. The border dispute was settled at the close of the year of 1757 by the Lords Commissioners of Trade of Great Britain. They established the border about where it is today. The New York-New Hampshire border was settled in 1791. After Vermont first declared itself a republic, it became the fourteenth state.

The Calico Indians

THE LORDS COMMISSIONERS OF TRADE ENDED THE BORDER DISPUTE, but that did not end the anti-rent matter in New York. Josiah Loomis and Robert Miller held meetings claiming Indian deeds to the area. They planned to file for grants for land that would bring the matter of ownership to court. Livingston dismissed the deeds as being from straggling Indians, and the Governor issued a proclamation for their arrest. More trouble broke out in 1766 with Robert Noble resulting in the loss of life. Noble was forced to flee, and this time detachments of infantry were stationed in the area to prevent him from returning.

Feelings against the landlords still ran high. Farmers still refused to pay rent. In 1791 Sheriff Hogeboom, of newly formed Columbia County, was shot and killed trying to hold a farm auction in Nobletown. He sent his deputy to hold an auction for Van Rensselaer, but because of protesters the deputy was forced to abandon the project. The following week, the Sheriff decided he would hold the auction himself. He went to the farm and waited, but his deputy failed to show up with the papers. After waiting, the sheriff said he would let it stand where it was. He started to ride off with his brother and another man. When he got opposite the barn, seventeen men dressed as Indians came out, and Jonathan Arnold, the farmer's son, fired a gun. They followed the sheriff, who walked his horse so as not to show fear. Then Arnold mounted a horse and caught up with them. He dismounted, aimed his gun, and shot the sheriff through the heart. The Sheriff's only words were "brother I am a dead man." Four of the men fled to Nova Scotia the next day. In the anti-rent movement this is the first instance the protesters dressed themselves as Indians.

In 1795 a petition was sent to the State Assembly asking to have the title of Livingston's investigated. It was based on the fact that Livingston claimed much more land than his deed called for. It was organized by Petrus Pulver and had more than 200 signers. They resented paying rent to the new heirs for the farms they settled. Opposition to Livingston's title was widespread but they still had political power. The petition was turned down.

The Livingstons, Van Rensselaers, and other speculators had vast holdings of land, and over the years, from the 1680s, had given leases similar to the lease of 1687, with the exception that the farmer promised to work the land for several generations instead of 10 years.

The feudal laws of Britain were important to how the manors worked. Inheritance law was that the oldest son had a right to inherit all. This kept the large estates intact. When a farmer died, if the younger sons got a share, the tenant's estate would have to be broken up. The question was if that happened, who would run the farm, and who would look after the widow? If the livestock, the tenant's major holding, were sold and the landlord collected his third, the profitability of the farm was in jeopardy. The landlord would have to find a new tenant. Alexander Hamilton drew up many of the later leases for his brother-in-law, Steven Van Rensselaer III. Hamilton, one of the framers of the Constitution, believed in a strong central government and in a ruling Aristocracy. One of his proposals for the Constitution was that the president be elected for life. His proposal is in a letter now in the Astor Library in New York.

Steven Van Rensselaer was also a Federalist and believed in the ruling aristocracy. They wanted to maintain the manor just as it operated before. Hamilton kept the leases within the letter of the law. The lease had a quarter-sale provision, giving the original owner the right to a quarter of the sale price if the leases were ever sold. The lease and the livestock usually passed to the farmer's oldest son by the farmer's will when he died. The farmer provided security for his wife by leaving her lifetime use of one room in the farmhouse. Because of these arrangements the farmer's son couldn't give up the farm. He was bound to the soil. After two or three lifetimes a new lease would have to be negotiated, but at a higher rent.

After the Revolution, soldiers who had been promised land were looking for a place to settle. The large estates taken over from the Tories had been sold to the well-connected speculators like the Van Rensselaers. Van Rensselaer would say to the soldiers, "you deserve a good start. Pick out a farm and I won't even charge you rent. Once you have it settled and it is producing, in four years come to me and I will give you 'durable' leases." There was, of course, only one lease; it was durable, and it included the requirement to pay all taxes and the old feudal custom of working for the landlord one day per year. The landlord also retained the right to all wood, minerals, water rights, and kept the quarter-sale provision. If the settler refused to sign, he was told to move on. Some did go West. Others stayed, probably to be near family.

Rent day was January 1st on the Van Rensselaer Manor. Every farmer had to come, and he was forced to wait in the cold until he was called to a small window to turn in his receipts for wheat and so forth that were delivered to the manor store or warehouse. If he could not pay, he had to sign a note. When Steven Van Rensselaer III died in 1839, his will directed all past-due rents be collected. That meant all the notes were due. When his heirs forced more foreclosures, farmers started to question the fairness of the leases, and how the landlords got the land. In Columbia County the dispute with the Livingstons and Van Rensselaers had been going on since about 1750, but now many new voices were added to the protest.

The most important man in the anti-rent movement in Rensselaer County at that time was a country doctor named Dr. Smith A. Boughton. His father was a tenant farmer so he knew the hardships of the tenant farmer firsthand. As a country doctor he was also in their houses every day. Around 1840, anti-rent meetings and protests started over a large area. It included Albany, Columbia, Dutchess, Delaware, Herkimer, Oneita, Otsego, Montgomery, Schoarie, Greene, Rensselear, and Ulster Counties. Doctor Boughton was a principle speaker in the eastern counties and, like the others, dressed as a Calico Indian. He used the name "Big Thunder" when he needed to keep his identity secret. The result was that more farmers refused to pay rent, and they pressured their neighbors not to pay.

As Dr. Boughton's fame spread, people like John I. Johnson, John Bain, and the Finkles, the leaders in Columbia County, traveled to meet with him and made plans. A way to communicate quickly was needed so they could react. They came up with the idea of using the tin dinner horn. Small farmers, too poor to own a bell, used the tin horn to call workers from the fields at dinner. They prohibited using the horn except as a signal that the sheriff was coming. They formed cells of ten Indians with the chief of each ten knowing the identity of only his ten. Some places formed insurance companies. If the sheriff sold the stock, the horses or cows would be shot before they could be taken away. The original owner would receive the value of the stock and of course the Van Rensselears received nothing. More often, the sheriff would find himself overpowered, his papers taken, and he would receive a coat of tar and feathers.

Big Thunder, Big Trouble

I LOOKED DOWN FROM MY HILL, AND I COULD SEE THE STORES, THE hotels, and the little town square where the roads all come together in a haphazard way. My great grandfather, Grant Darius Langdon, built the general store in 1890. His store dominates one corner, and is one of the newer buildings. The village had its public well along the road and close to the store. In earlier days it offered a hardy farmer's wife a place to water the horse before returning home. When I was growing up there was a wooden memorial next to the then closed well. It was put up after World War I and listed those who died in the Civil War and the Great War. Over the well stood a movable frame that held the coming movie poster for the theater on the south edge of the village. The McIntire family built the theater on land purchased from my farm in my grandfather's time. It was part of the way of life until it was burned by a serial arsonist a few years back. CNN News came to cover the fear the community felt as they wondered who would be next. The arsonist burned three of my barns and scores of other buildings and was never caught. As a young boy in the days before television, I always strained to see what the next movie would be as we rode past the movie poster in the car. A flagpole stood in the center of the square then that had a curb and grass. This square has changed remarkably little in the last hundred years, except for the town clock that replaced the flagpole and the memorial after World War II. The McIntyre family gave the clock in honor of their son, Steven. Across the street from the store is the hotel that Grant Darius Langdon also owned. Back in his time, Copake was a lively little town on a Saturday night when the ore diggers from the iron mines came to town. Hunting and fishing were also important and attracted sporting parties to the hotel. Fishing tackle was available in the store and the hotel had dogs available for sporting parties that stayed there. The area had railroad service, and the hotel had a livery that now serves as the drug store. The Sweets also ran a racetrack on the north edge of the village. Before the days of refrigeration, the butcher went up and down the roads selling fresh meat, and other peddlers also came by. It was a pleasant way of life. The biggest change came back in the 1920s when the state came through and paved the state road. The residents got together and had them pave the road past the church and put in sidewalks.

The old Holsapple House was known as Sweet's Hotel back in 1844, and is on another corner of the square across from the store. John S. Livingston, one of the heirs to the manor, owned nearly all the farms around the village back then. He was having trouble collecting his rent, and that is why Sheriff Henry Miller came in his buggy into the square at Copake. He had papers in his pocket to sell enough livestock to pay the rent. The square was bigger then because the store on the corner and the new church still had not been built.

The Taghkanic Mutual Association that included leaders like the Finkles, John Bain, and John I. Johnson had things well planned. Abram Vosburgh and Steven Decker would refuse to pay rent to John Livingston. They knew Livingston would have papers drawn up, and they would have to be served. The auction was advertised. The year was 1844; it was December 11 and they knew the sheriff would be coming to serve the papers. The sheriff had made arrangements to meet his deputy, Walter Shaver, at Sweet's Hotel the day before. They were going out to serve the papers together. But, The Taghkanic Mutual Association had planned things carefully with their members; and Dr. Smith Boughten, Big Thunder, was there. He came down from Rensselaer County for the event.

When Sheriff Miller left Hudson he was alone and was unconcerned as he drove along in his buggy. When he arrived in Copake he knew something was up. Ever since he left Hudson he heard the sound of a tin dinner horn blowing when he drove past a farm. Then he would hear other horns further and further away. At the next farm he would hear the sound again. Soon he noticed people began to follow him. By the time he got to Copake, the people following had grown to a large crowd, and he could not turn back. In town, people were coming in from all directions. It was the largest number of people to ever crowd into the small square. It was the most significant event to take place there. The Calico Indians of the Taghkanic Mutual Association had carefully planned what was about to take place. It seemed the entire county knew, but no one told the sheriff.

One estimate was there were 500 farmers dressed as Indians in bright calico costumes. They had their faces painted or covered with sheep skin masks so no one could recognize them. A thousand spectators also crowded around to see what was going to happen. The sheriff was highly concerned at this point. He tried to slip through the crowd into the hotel by the side door to meet his deputy. Eight Indians crowded through the door behind him. Inside, Big Thunder gave the order to draw arms, and the sheriff was in the middle of the group with guns pointed at him from every direction. Big Thunder spoke, "Is the Sheriff of Columbia County in the room?" Sheriff Miller said, "I am the man." Big Thunder said, "I am the chief of the Indians. We have assembled to prevent the sale. We want to do it peaceably if we can, but if we cannot...." What happened then was not recorded. A door was shut. Because of the large crowd the sheriff had few choices.

Later, Big Thunder escorted Miller and Shaver to their wagon. "You will go no faster than the procession. The Indians will move with the music to the place of sale," he told the sheriff. "Little Thunder will precede your horses, and a hollow square will be formed around you." Then the small band that the Calico Indians had assembled for the task struck up a march, and Big Thunder strode out in front.

They reached the Vosburgh farm a mile and a half down the road and the procession stopped. The sheriff said, "I must sell the property as advertised." Big Thunder said, "If you attempt to sell today, you do it at your own peril. We have met to prevent the sale. We'll do it at all hazards."

The sheriff then said, "I will not attempt to sell." Then he added, "I must go on to the Decker Farm," and the procession went on.

At the Decker farm the sheriff got out. Steven Decker was in the yard. He asked Steven Decker if he was prepared to pay.

Decker told him, "No, you will have to go ahead and sell."

Big and Little Thunder both drew their pistols. Big Thunder said, "If you do, you do so at your peril."

The sheriff then climbed back into the wagon. Big Thunder said, "You can't go yet. It is the custom of the Indian Chief to take from the sheriff all papers dealing with rents."

"I will not give up my papers until I am satisfied that those around me are determined to commit violence," Miller said.

"I can satisfy you on that very quickly," Big Thunder replied, "Natives, give heed! The sheriff is unwilling to give up his papers unless satisfied we are ready to take them by force. All in favor raise your left hand."

Every Indian hand went up, and a war whoop echoed in the valley. The other spectators were then asked if they agreed and they shouted their assent. The papers were handed over, and Steven Decker got into the wagon with the sheriff, and they headed back to town.

Back in town someone placed a pile of straw in the road and another brought a pail of brandy from the hotel, and they started passing it around. At this point, the sheriff joined in. Big Thunder poked the straw with his sword and said, "Palefaces, is there any danger of burning the tavern if we fire this?"

"Fire it," they shouted.

Big Thunder then burned the papers, and they sang a chorus of "Big Bill Snyder" to the tune of "Old Dan Tucker." Bill Snyder was a hard drinking, rough deputy sheriff in Albany County and was run off by the "Indians" when he went out to serve papers on a farmer. Later someone brought out a straw dummy and they burned John Livingston in effigy. Big Thunder assured the crowd the sheriff of Columbia County was "as good an anti-renter as you are." The Indians took the sheriff into the hotel and purchased his dinner. Later the brandy flowed in an upstairs room where it couldn't be observed.

I own two old pistols. I like to refer to them as the guns that won the West. It isn't that they were ever in the West, but they and thousands like them had an impact on how the West was settled. They were used in the Anti-Rent War and helped bring land reform to the United States. One has brass parts and the other is iron with the trigger guard missing. One belonged to Abraham R. Vosburgh, my great, great, grandfather, the other to John Vosburgh, Abraham's brother, who later moved to Wisconsin. They were carried that day in Copake to confront Sheriff Miller. Because Abram Vosburgh was apparently not at home when the sheriff called to serve papers, it has led me to speculate that he was one of the eight that crowded into Sweet's Tavern with Sheriff Miller. Since Miller didn't ask for Abraham Vosburgh when he got to the farm it leaves me wondering if the sheriff knew he was one of the eight. It will never be known for sure.

Smoky Hollow

THE LEADERS CALLED A MEETING IN SMOKY HOLLOW (HOLLOWVILLE) on December 18, 1844 following the incident in Copake. The Taghkanic Mutual Association was formally organized in November to coordinate resistance to the payment of rent. John I. Johnson was the president and most of the meetings were held at the home of James Yager, at Taghkanic. Members disguised themselves as Calico Indians to keep their identity secret when they went to meetings. They had five vice presidents, James M. Strever, Samual A. Tanner, George L. Finkle, George I. Rossman, and Peter Poucher. Philip B. Miller was the treasurer, Anthony Poucher was recording secretary, and Peter Poucher was corresponding secretary. John Bain and James M. Strever served on the executive committee. The Association had the support of nearly all of the farmers. Feeling ran very high in the community. There was no middle ground. If you didn't support the movement or passed information along to the Livingstons, your neighbor and friends might burn your barn. Old friendships meant nothing if it got in the way of the fight against the landlords. If you resisted openly, you had to suffer the wrath of the Livingstons.

John I. Johnson and his executive committee were delighted with how the Copake event went off. There wasn't a hitch. The sheriff had no idea what was happening, yet the entire county knew, and no one talked. All of their meetings and planning paid off. No one was hurt, and the landlord was beaten. He couldn't collect the rent. The word spread like wild fire to all the farms up and down the Hudson Valley. The Association leaders sensed the time was right to strike again. This was just the beginning. Now was the time to have another meeting.

The Smoky Hollow meeting was bigger than the Copake affair. There were 3,000 people and 200 Calico Indians. Dr. Boughton, dressed as Big Thunder, was the main speaker. He wanted to inform the crowd of progress in organizing the other counties and build a strong united front. Dr. Boughton hoped to attract enough support to land the matter of rent in the courts.

He started out from Rensselaer County before sunrise that morning to meet the executive committee and other leaders at Miller's Tavern. The crowd of about 3,000 tenants gathered outside while the leaders talked. About mid-afternoon 200 Calico Indians rode up giving war hoops and some in the crowd blew tin horns. When the meeting was about to start, Big Thunder came out. William Rifenburgh, a young man from Hillsdale, was standing right in front of Big Thunder. A shot rang out, and Rifenburgh was shot dead. It didn't stop the meeting, but it did put a damper on things. It was speculated that the shot was intended for Big Thunder, and the sheriff never attempted to find who was responsible. The death was ruled accidental.

The landlords knew they had to stop this movement right away. The pressure of the Livingstons and Van Rensselaers was felt through the prodding Joseph D. Monell, whom the Governor elect was expected to make Surrogate of the county, and the District Attorney. They accompanied the sheriff to arrest Dr. Boughton when his identity was discovered after the meeting. He was accused of taking the sheriff's papers in Copake and destroying them. The Doctor resisted arrest and made a break for it. A scuffle took place and the Doctor, for a time, held the sheriff at bay with his gun. He was finally talked into custody when the sheriff promised bail. They promised him a hearing at eleven o'clock the next morning if he went peaceably. The Doctor, Little Thunder, and Samuel Wheeler, a local leader, were arrested that night.

The next morning the landlords made their political power felt. The Governor came down hard on the farmers. The hearing was called off. The lawyers for the defendants got an order from Supreme Court Commissioner Dorr of Hillsdale ordering another hearing to set bail. The Governor issued an order blocking the hearing and removing Supreme Court Commissioner Russell Dorr of Hillsdale from office. He called on the Attorney General, John Van Buren, to prosecute the case. John was the son of former President Martin Van Buren. Martin Van Buren lost the election of 1840, but still had political ambitions, as did his son. They needed the landlords' support. Big Thunder would get a day in court, but it was for burning the sheriff's papers in Copake and not over the ownership of land. Dr. Boughten, Mortimer Belden, who was Little Thunder, and Samuel Wheeler, a local leader, were kept without bail in the Hudson jail. The farmers that expected them to be set free on bail had come to escort the prisoners home the next day. When they weren't released they stayed and burned fires on the hills around Hudson. The Mayor was scared the farmers would storm the jail to free the prisoners. He declared a state of emergency and called in state troops to protect the city. He called on local supporters to protect the city and back the landlords' interests. Meanwhile, 10 other local leaders were rounded up and jailed for their involvement. When the Governor removed Dorr it stirred the farmers' emotions on the other side. They called a meeting at Churchtown and had former Commissioner Dorr as a speaker. He sided with the farmers but warned them not to do anything that would push public support away from their cause. To the farmers, the administration of the laws was unjust and corrupted by politics.

"Prince John" Van Buren sided with the politically powerful landlords. The former president attended the trial to show his support for his son and the politically powerful landlords. Dr. Boughten was tried separately and was defended by New York lawyer Ambrose L. Jordan. The Judge was Judge Amasa J. Parker, and the trial lasted three weeks. The jury stood 11 to 1 for acquittal, so the trial ended in a mistrial.

After the mistrial, bail was again denied, and a new judge was sent for. The new Judge was Judge Edmonds, a personal friend of both Governor Wright and Martin Van Buren. Governor Wright had appointed him to the circuit bench in New York. Judge Edmons had started his law practice in Van Buren's law office and knew most of the people in the county. He was openly friendly to Prince John and boasted he would "convict Big Thunder in short order."

The first thing Judge Edmonds did was exclude all farmers from the jury pool. When John Van Buren moved to admit some new evidence it was too much for Jordan. A series of insults broke out. Ambrose Jordan accused John of not caring about justice but only his own ambitions and building his own reputation. Finally a heated argument erupted, and the two lawyers wound up in a fistfight. The two lawyers had to spend the night in jail, and the Judge had to call off his planned dinner party at Lindenwald with the ex-president. The lawyers apologized the next day, and then the trial went on. The Doctor and Little Thunder were finally found guilty in the fall. Little Thunder's health was already broken by the harsh imprisonment by this time. Judge Edmonds handed down a harsh sentence. He sentenced them both to life in prison but the other anti-renters were given lesser sentences. The doctor was put on a boat at Hudson and was sent up river to Albany on the way to Dannamora. When the boat carrying Dr. Boughten and Mortimer Belden reached Albany they were afraid to dock because of a huge crowd of friendly supporters that came to see the Doctor. They sent the boat on to Troy. The landlords, of course, were pleased with the stiff sentences. A joke of the day was, "why is John Van Buren like Benjamin Franklin?" The answer was, "Franklin bottled lightning, and Van Buren bottled Thunder."

With Big Thunder in jail the landlords made a big push to enforce the law statewide. Another big incident happened in Delaware County when Deputy Osman Steel was killed trying to sell stock owned by Moses Earle. The authorities attempted to arrest every Indian at the auction and hold them all guilty of murder. In Delhi, the county had to build extra log jails to house all the prisoners. Again farmers were excluded from the jury pool, and harsh sentences were handed down.

According to Christman's book, *Tin Horns and Calico*, things finally changed for the farmers. There was a political backlash. Public opinion went in favor of the farmers because of the harsh sentences. The anti-rent press stirred up public support for the farmers. Alvin Bovay, Thomas Devyr, Horace Greeley, and others gave support to the farmers in their newspapers. The battle was

taken to the ballot box. The old Federalist Party of Hamilton and
Steven Van Rensselaer had vanished by this time. They were seen
as pro-British during the War of 1812. The new party that formed
after the Federalist Party was the Whigs. The two leading political parties of the time were the Whig and the Democratic Parties. The Democratic Party of Jefferson and Jackson was split
between the Barnburners and the Hunkers. The Hunkers advocated a liberal spending policy, and the Barnburners, like John
Van Buren and Govenor Silas Wright, were conservative on
spending. Van Buren was anti-slave. The farmers were tradition-
ally democratic at this time. When it was clear the farmers were
going to vote their interest and formed their own political party,
both parties tried to attract their vote. The anti-renters became
allied in the press with the Free Soil Party that was against slavery
in any new states.

Governor Wright sensed trouble. In January of 1846 he took
up the anti-rent cause by asking the legislature to "rid the state
of the ghost of feudalism." He asked that a commission be
formed headed by Samuel Tilden, a distinguished lawyer from
New Lebanon, Columbia County. Tilden's father was a well-
known farmer and merchant who settled there about 1790. He
was a good friend of his neighbor Martin Van Buren. Samuel was
sent to Yale University and grew up knowing Van Buren and other
leading politicians. He was known for his integrity. He later served
as Governor and was the Democratic candidate for president in
1876 against Rutherford B. Hayes. Tilden won almost 52% of the
popular vote but lost the electoral vote by just one vote. His commission came down on the side of land reform. They recommended destruction of the manors. The commission wanted to
limit leases to 10 years and to break up the estates on the death of
the owners. It also wanted to make them pay taxes.

In June of 1846 a Constitutional Convention was called with 53 of the delegates farmers or mechanics. With slavery becoming an issue, the Democratic Party was split; some Democrats quoted the Bible to prove Negroes belonged in an inferior social position. The anti-renters, who were in a socially inferior position, believed position should be awarded on merit, integrity, and ability without regard to race or social position. The anti-renters wanted to end old Federalism of the elite class as well as feudalism. The constitution they proposed was much more democratic than the old "Federalist" Constitution of 1777, which had already been revised. The original constitution required ownership of 100 acres of land free of debt to vote.

The new constitution called for land reform. It prohibited issuing any more feudal leases. It outlawed some provisions of existing leases, such as the quarter sale and similar restraints on transfer of title. It limited agricultural leases to 12 years. Eventually the matter was taken to court and the anti-renters won. The new Constitution held up in court.

In 1848, John Slingerlands, the anti-rent congressman, proposed a Homestead Act that placed the idea of free land for the common man on the national agenda. The southern aristocrats defeated it.

Western Expansion

Aɴᴅʀᴇᴡ Jᴀᴄᴋsoɴ ᴡᴀs ᴋɴowɴ ᴀs Oʟᴅ Hɪᴄᴋoʀʏ ʙᴇᴄᴀᴜsᴇ ʜᴇ ʜᴀᴅ an unbending will. He was fair but very tough and demanding. His winning of the battle of New Orleans and high-spirited actions like getting involved in barroom fights and duels inspired people. He encouraged the Western growth of the nation. He liked the West because it was a place a person of humble beginnings like himself could get ahead. It was a place where the amount of money and influence your family had didn't count as much as your ability to get things done. People started talking about Manifest Destiny, the expansion of the nation to the Pacific.

Texas was part of Mexico when Robert R. Livingston purchased Louisiana during the Jefferson administration in 1803. Texas only had a population of about 7,000 people then. Moses Austin played an important part in Texas history. He was a New England Yankee born in Durham, Connecticut. He moved south and operated lead mines in Virginia and then Missouri, but in 1819 he lost his money. He was looking for a way to start over when he got the right to settle on some land in Texas from the

Spanish government. He died before he could go there and start his project, but his son, Stephen, took it over in 1821 and settled 300 families. The Mexican government made more grants to Americans, and by 1830 about 25,000 Americans lived there. Then problems began to break out in Mexico. General Santa Anna abolished the Mexican Constitution and declared himself dictator. This caused an uprising, and Texas declared independence from Mexico in 1836. The fight for Texas independence and the death of former three-term Tennessee congressman and frontier hero, Davy Crockett, at the Alamo excited the American imagination. Crockett had served under Andrew Jackson in the Indian wars and was elected colonel of the militia. He was a frontier character like no other and had served a year as an indentured servant as a youth. He had little education, was plainspoken, and was a better hunter than a frontier farmer. His tall stories of the frontier in a book published in Cincinnati made him a popular politician hero for the common man. As a congressman he introduced a bill to give free land to the frontier farmer. The aristocrats easily defeated it. He owed his initial popularity to Jackson, but he broke with Jackson on the issue of the National Bank and the resettlement of the Indians. When he broke with Jackson it cost him votes and he lost the election. After he lost the election he went to Texas where he was killed at the Alamo. President Martin Van Buren didn't want war with Mexico and opposed the annexation of Texas. Van Buren didn't want another slave state. Finally, President Tyler obtained a resolution calling for the annexation of Texas. Texas was admitted as a state in 1845.

James K. Polk was elected president in 1844 and took office in 1845. He was an excellent orator and was elected to Jackson's old seat in Tennessee. He idolized Jackson so much so that they called him Young Hickory. He added a million square miles to the country and was the president responsible for the expansion of the United States to the Pacific. He first tried to purchase California from Mexico but was turned down. The exact location of the border between Texas and Mexico was a problem, so in 1846 he used the boundary issue to declare war on Mexico. The Mexican War ended in 1848, and the United States gained more territory. The Texas border was placed at the Rio Grande, and the United States was allowed to purchase Mexico's northern Providence of California and New Mexico. The United States paid Mexico 15 million dollars and assumed certain debts owed its citizens.

Polk also settled the Oregon boundary with Britain. Britain claimed the Columbia River in 1792. Lewis and Clark explored there in 1805 as part of the Louisiana Purchase, and in 1811, John Jacob Astor established his Astoria fur trading post there. In 1818 the United States agreed with Britain to jointly occupy this area as others also claimed some land in the area. Then Spain gave up its claim above California and Russia its claim to all but Alaska. By 1843, enough settlers came over the Oregon Trail to set up a government near Salem, Oregon. The unsettled border became a problem in the election of 1844. James Polk made it an issue with a campaign slogan of 54–40 or fight. A compromise was reached, and the border to the north was settled in 1846. The Oregon Territory was established in 1848. Congress wanted to encourage settlement, so they passed the Donation Land Act to give land to new settlers that would move there.

All this new land came with a problem; that was the what to do about the old problem of slavery. The question was, should slavery be permitted on the new land or did the Missouri Compromise of 1820 prohibit slavery in the new territories? The Generals in the field decided the outcome of the Civil War, but it was the politicians that made the decision that war would be fought.

When the Revolution took place, laws were needed to take the place of the British laws of the time. Many of the old feudal laws and customs of Britain were used. Slavery was one of these laws. When the Constitution was adapted, it recognized slavery by the way Representatives were chosen. Five slaves were counted as three people in choosing members of the House of Representatives. While some states in the North already stopped the practice, The British Empire didn't outlaw slavery until 1833. It had been under a death warrant for years, and many of the Northern slaves were sent to the cotton South and an eager market. The 1820 census shows the slave population of the North at 18,001, mostly in New York and New Jersey. In 1830, the number dropped to just 2,779, nearly all in New Jersey. Of the 10,000 that were dropped from the census in New York, some likely got jobs, some too old to work lived in poverty, and others no doubt were sold South. New York still was listed as having 75 slaves in 1830 even though slavery was outlawed. They were probably older slaves that continued to live with the family because they had no other place to go. The total slave population of the country increased by 570,597 in that same ten-year period. The states of South Carolina, Georgia, Alabama, and Tennessee had the biggest increase. When the British ended slavery, it aided the anti-slave movement in this country and helped fuel the controversy. South Carolina was one of those states having a feudal constitution giving the power to the plantation owners. The value of their slaves made them rich. They had already threatened to secede in 1828 over high tariffs that protected the Northern industry. Slavery was a new issue to cause problems.

Zachary Taylor was the hero of the Mexican War and was the Whig candidate for President in 1848. Martin Van Buren was one of the Democrats upset over the South's push to extend slavery in the West. The Free Soil Party opposed the extension of slavery in the new territories. Van Buren left the Democratic Party to run for president for the Free Soil Party in 1848. Van Buren pulled enough votes in New York from Democrat Luis Cass to give Zachary Taylor the Presidency. Taylor was our last slave-owning President and was a no-nonsense army General that believed in the Union. He was born in Virginia to an aristocratic family that moved to a plantation near Louisville, Kentucky when he was young. He felt slavery was needed in cotton growing areas, but should be prohibited in other areas. He was different from the Southern Democrats on that point. He was for allowing California to be admitted as a free state. Others from the South saw this as a violation of the Missouri Compromise of 1820. They said because it was below 36 degrees 30 minutes, Congress should insist it be a slave state. South Carolina threatened to secede, but President Taylor, a Southerner, told them he would invade them to preserve the Union. The Compromise of 1850 was worked out to appease the South by making the fugitive slave laws stronger. Taylor opposed The Compromise and probably would have vetoed it, but he died in July of 1850. Millard Fillmore became President and The Compromise was passed and the nation edged toward the Civil War.

In 1854 the Kansas-Nebraska Act was passed creating a new territory that stretched to the Canadian border. The sponsors of the bill were Stephen Douglas and Andrew Buttler from South Carolina. Douglas, born in Vermont, was the senator from Illinois. He was for Western expansion and was looking for land for the transcontinental railroad. He knew the bill would cause political trouble, but he wanted a northern route from Chicago over a southern route. He needed that territory opened up to get land for his route. He was willing to give a clear victory to the plantation owners who wanted to extend slavery in order to get their support for the

Act. President Pierce, a lawyer from New Hampshire, backed the bill, and Congress repealed the Missouri Compromise of 1820. The Missouri Compromise was worked out to admit Maine and Missouri as states and to keep an even balance of slave and non-slave states in 1820. One of its provisions prohibited slavery north of 36 degree 30 minutes, which meant it had to be repealed. The Kansas-Nebraska Act gave the settlers the right to decide if the new territory was to be slave or free. Land was sold by the government at the time in blocks of 640 acres at $1.25 per acre, which was large for small farmers of the North who lacked capital to hire workers. After it was put up for bids for two weeks it could be divided into smaller lots, but by then the better land was usually gone. The small farmers could not compete with the cheap labor. The small farmer saw slavery as a tool of the aristocrats, one they couldn't afford. The rich and powerful still made the rules.

A lot of wealthy plantation owners came to Kansas. Cotton and their cheap slave labor made them rich. They had capital in the form of slaves that they brought along and could work large farms easily. They looked down on the farmers from the North that plowed their own fields and never had the privileged up-bringing that came with their wealth. In Kansas, the slave interest won the first election. Then a battle broke out because the free men refused to recognize the government and set up their own government. Two of John Brown's sons were among the anti-slave settlers, and when he joined them many bitter fights and battles took place. The free men won the second election, and Kansas became a free state. The wealthy plantation owners of the South who controlled the politics there didn't like the second election. Some of them had made large investments in land, counting on their slaves to do the work, and they felt their interest was threatened.

The Kansas-Nebraska Bill caused a lot of political trouble in the North. The Kansas-Nebraska Bill was seen as another victory for the southern aristocrats and slavery. The small farmer could only afford small farms, but there were a lot of them. These farmers had no tradition of slavery. They saw themselves doing the same tasks as the slaves only on the poorer soils. It was the age-old struggle of the rich against the poor. This feeling nourished the formation of the Republican Party. Quite a few anti-renters from New York moved to Wisconsin. They included people like John Vosburgh and others from Copake area, but some prominent ones too. According to Christman's book *Tin Horns and Calico*, two prominent anti-rent leaders were Alvin Bovay, publisher of anti-rent newspapers back in New York, and Amos Loper. They signed the meeting notice in 1854 in Ripon, Wisconsin calling for the formation of a new party. They brought with them the idea of giving land to the people who did the work of settling it. Free land was very popular on the western frontier with its large number of small farmers. These farmers resented the privileged class of the South just as they resented the privileged like Livingston back East. The southern planters needed large farms to make use of the slave labor. They were bitterly opposed to free land for small farms.

The push for free land came from the Northern small farms as the sons moved west looking for farms to settle. They didn't have capital and had to borrow money from rich Eastern banks. They became the backbone of the Republican Party. They nominated Freemont of California for President in 1854. He was an explorer of the West, and gold on his California estate made him rich. He ran on a mild anti-slave platform to keep slavery out of the new territories. Millard Fillmore was the Whig candidate, and he represented business and the new aristocrats of the South. Buchanan was from Pennsylvania and ran as the Democrat. He was pro-slave and backed the Kansas-Nebraska Act. As a Jackson Democrat, Buchanan held onto enough of the farm votes to win easily. The slave interests were split, but they still out-polled Freemont.

When Buchanan became president he faced all kinds of problems. The trouble earlier in Kansas with John Brown leading raids to free Kansas of slavery was one. When slavery was defeated in the second Kansas election, South Carolina threatened to secede. Then the Supreme court handed down the Dred Scott Decision in 1857, which Buchanan backed. It said Congress had no right to prohibit slavery in any territory.

Dred Scott was a slave that was taken into a free territory by his owner. After three years he sued to gain his freedom. This decision, while it didn't recognize Scott's right to sue, gave slave owners the right to take their slaves anywhere in the country. This infuriated the small farmers of the North. The small New York farmer just threw off the yoke of the Livingstons and Van Rensselaers and such. To them slavery was a tool of the rich, and it wasn't clear slaves couldn't be brought into any state and even New York.

The Civil War

In the 1860 election there were four candidates with the Democrats split into North and South over the slave issue. The Northern Democrats ran Stephen Douglas and the Southern Democrats ran Vice President Breckinridge from Kentucky. Breckinridge was pro-slave. The other southern candidate was John Bell of Tennessee, who tried to ignore the slave issue.

The Republicans of the North didn't even run in 10 southern states and nominated Abraham Lincoln. Lincoln was born in the slave state of Kentucky, but he disliked slavery and had worked his way up from poverty. He adapted a mild stand on slavery. He was for enforcing the fugitive slave law but kept the plank excluding slavery in the new territories. Douglas was the main opponent to Lincoln in the northern states. Douglas's problem with the farm vote was his Kansas-Nebraska Act and Popular Sovereignty. Lincoln came out strongly for a Pacific Railroad, but what won him support of the small northern farmers was his support of the Homestead Act. I believe the small farmer won Lincoln the election, not his mild stand on slavery. The anti-slave people didn't like Douglas, so they helped, but it was the farm vote that delivered the most votes.

Senator Andrew Johnson of Tennessee favored the small farmer over the aristocrats of the South who wanted to expand slavery. Johnson was a southerner, but he was far from an aristocrat. He was born in North Carolina. His father died when he was young, so there was no money for school. He was hired out as an apprentice to a tailor, which he hated. When he was in his teens he moved to Tennessee, married, and opened his own tailorshop before going into politics. He was elected to Congress in 1843 and became a senator in 1857. He, like Jackson, grew up in poverty and represented the common man of the South and frontier. When he saw free homesteads as an issue for farmers he introduced a Homestead Act as a congressman. It went nowhere. Just before the 1860 election the now Senator Johnson wrote a compromise Homestead Bill. He hoped to hold the small farmer vote for the Democrats. Johnson got his bill passed, but the southern aristocrats opposed the bill, and South Carolina was talking about secession again. The Democratic President, James Buchanan from Pennsylvania, vetoed it. It was a blunder. Buchanan was trying to appease the aristocrats of South Carolina and hold the Union together. He lost the farm vote for the Democrats though, including the northern Democrat candidate, Steven Douglas.

The Homestead Act became an important campaign issue. The small northern farmers kept voting for Jackson's Democrats, but when the Homestead Act was vetoed they changed. It wasn't the cry of "free the slaves" that won Lincoln the election, it was the cry of "free land." His stand to limit the spread of slavery lost him support in the South, of course, and his failure to even run in the South was probably a mistake. If he just got some support from the small southern farmer it would have made it harder for the South to secede for the Union. He didn't need that support to win though. It was Lincoln that was the champion of the common man over the interest of the aristocrats. He carried every northern state against Douglas except for New Jersey. Lincoln won the election in the North against Stephen A. Douglas, the Democrat of the North, by a landslide. Lincoln won 59% of the electoral vote. He got 180 electoral votes to Douglas's 12. The South went for Breckinridge with 72 votes and Bell with 39 votes. Lincoln had Hannibal Hamlin from Maine as vice president; Douglas had Herschel V. Johnson from Georgia as his vice presidential candidate, Breckinridge had Lane from Oregon, and Bell had Evertt from Massachusetts.

After Abraham Lincoln became president, the Civil War started. The Civil War was more than just a battle over the ownership of Black men's souls; it was a war of two worlds and what to do with the western land. It was the aristocratic feudal-embraced world of the South against the new order emerging in the North. In his book, *The Great Republic,* Sir Winston Churchill estimated 3,000 to 4,500 slave owners controlled the politics of the South. The new order was the common man of the Andrew Jackson era in the North. It was the land-reforming tenant farmers like those of the Taconic Hills, and it was the frontier settlers like those in Wisconsin. In the North, with more people, the common people of New York were already victorious over the landed aristocrats. To understand what happened, it helps to understand the times and to remember who Lincoln was and where he came from. He married Mary Todd of Louisville, Kentucky. The Todds were an aristocratic, well-connected family. The people around Louisville said that the Todds spelled their name with two Ds, but one D was enough for God. Lincoln, though, was a man of the frontier, born poor in the slave state of Kentucky. His father was a younger son, so under English law, his older brother had inherited everything including slaves. When his father tried to make a living as a small farmer, he couldn't compete with the large plantations with slaves. The settlers around Lincoln were young men from the small farms and towns of New England, New York, and such. Lincoln was for the small farmer but he was not running on a platform to eliminate slavery. He didn't like slavery, but as a lawyer he supported the fugitive slave law and did work for the railroads. When Lincoln won, the wealthy plantation owners of the South felt disenfranchised because slavery would be limited. Lincoln was a Northerner and he didn't bother to run in the South. Lincoln didn't owe the South any political favors. The southern politicians knew the programs Lincoln would introduce would favor the small farmer and wouldn't help them in their interest of extending slavery. The sale of surplus slaves to the new lands was an important source of income. Some farmers sold horses, others sold slaves.

The political power of the United States was now centered in the more populated North. To Lincoln, the Civil War was the war to preserve the Union. Lincoln was born in 1809, and his history of the United States was of the Revolution when the colonies had to unite to win their independence. The motto "United We Stand, Divided We Fall" still hung heavy in the air in Lincoln's youth. Lincoln felt that if Kentucky seceded, the war would be lost. His close advisor in Louisville was Robert Breckinridge, brother of presidential candidate John C. Breckinridge who fought with the Confederacy.

After the Civil War started, the powerful southern plantation interest was no longer represented in Congress. The only southerner to remain in Congress was senator, and future president, Andrew Johnson of Tennessee. He stayed with the Union, not to free the slaves, but to preserve the Union, and smite the old feudal order of the South. To him it was the war, not just to save the Union, but to gain equal rights for the common man. The Homestead Act was introduced and passed easily this time, and Lincoln signed the Homestead Act of 1862 into law. At last, you only needed to file a claim, build a house, and then live on it for five years to obtain a 160-acre homestead. Johnson was known as a War Democrat because of his strong support for the Union and the fact he didn't resign and go with his state. Because of his loyalty, he became Lincoln's choice for Vice President in his second term. He replaced Hamlin from Maine. Johnson became our seventeenth president when Lincoln died. His southern origins probably caused much of his trouble with the Northern Congress, but he may have been a good choice for this very difficult time. Andrew Johnson is looked on by many historians as a racist, and one of our lower-rated presidents. Yet he was chosen by Lincoln to take the reins of government. It was that decision by the Kentucky born Lincoln that helped heal the wounds of war. The wounds would not heal for a hundred years but healing was started by the policy of inclusion. The South had some input at the top.

For many it was a chance to start a new life. It was the first time the new Republic gave land to the common man in mass. Many of the early settlers were the sons of tenant farmers in the East and couldn't raise the $1.25 per acre called for by the Land Act of 1820. They had to borrow money from, and were beholden to, the Eastern interest. Others just became squatters. They found an area and began farming it without the benefit of a title. They worked hard to establish their homestead. Breaking the thick prairie sod for the first time was hard work and required special plows. It was attractive for speculators to come in and make a legal claim on the new farms after they were improved. In 1841 the government granted Squatters Rights, giving them the right to purchase the land at the minimum price. Speculators, however, still came in and purchased it without giving adequate notice. The eastern farmer and new immigrants liked the Homestead Act so much so that they settled 50 million acres of the West in 20 years. In the 40 years after passage of the Homestead Act the population of the country doubled. In 1889 the government compelled the Creeks and the Seminoles to sell unsettled parts of their land. On April 22, 1889 the Oklahoma District was opened to settlement under the Homestead Act. Within a half day, 1,920,000 acres were claimed. The unoccupied Cherokee Outlet was opened up in 1893, and 100,000 settlers entered the area in a single day.

The Homestead Act was important to development of the West, but the land Congress gave the railroads was more important. Those with influence and power still did well. Congress loved to give huge land subsidies to the railroads to develop the transportation in the West, and the railroad grants became the basis of some of America's great fortunes. Between 1850 and 1871, Congress gave an area three times the size of Pennsylvania to various companies to build railroads. They gave 40 million acres for the building of the Union Pacific and Central Pacific Railroads alone. The railroad grants were usually given as every other section of 640 acres. Some were two and three sections deep creating a checkerboard appearance. Congress gave land to the railroads but it also benefited the government. It was a vast country with millions of acres of undeveloped land. When a railroad was built, transportation became cheaper, and the land near the railroad became more valuable, including the land the government kept. The land given to the Illinois Central is a good example. The company was given 4,055 square miles of land, 2,595,200 acres, an area nearly the size of Connecticut. That same land had been offered for sale for 15 years at $1.25 per acre and found no buyers. The land was offered for sale in 1852 at

$2.50 per acre, and the railroad sold 2,509,120 acres on land warrants in the next 12 months. They sold 298,861 acres of it for cash. The sections of land between the railroad grants were still available to the homesteaders. Not all railroads were that successful, but the railroad was largely an American development. Even before the Civil War, the United States had most of the world's railroads. In 1857 the total miles of railroad in the world was 55,256, and the United States had 28,500 miles. The railroads sold the land right away. First of all, they needed the money to build the railroad and, secondly, it was the farmers that would be their customers for transportation and provide them with revenue. They even sent agents abroad to help make land sales in such countries of Europe as Sweden. That is why, even today, you will see a section of the country populated by Swedish people and so forth. The railroad land grants did a lot to develop the West; still, it was the land grants to the homesteaders that defined the American spirit. It was the government giving land to the common man and not just the rich and the railroad barons that set America apart after the Civil War. The Civil War not only ended slavery, but it ended the domination of the old aristocrats and brought about a new order. Free land, the cheap railroad land, and cheap rail transportation developed the West quickly. It cost $5.88 to transport a 196 pound barrel of flour 300 miles over land. The freight rate was 1 cent per mile for 100 pounds. That was more than the value of the flour. By rail, the same barrel of flour could be shipped from Cincinnati to New York for a dollar. All of the new agricultural production lowered the commodity prices, helped create demand for household goods and machinery, and drove the economy. This demand spurred industry and the invention and development of such things as the moldboard plow and the reaper. It also created a demand for more transportation.

In the 1600s, the first Lord of Livingston Manor, Robert Livingston, used the feudal English law and his political friends to acquire land and a staff of servants to build, clear, and work the farms of the manor. He lived well, kept the spoils of their labor, and returned little to the people who settled and worked his land. Just before the Civil War, the political movement for land reform that started around 1750 grew powerful enough to change the New York State Constitution. After the conflict was settled, the old manors were broken up, and the purchase of public land was no longer at the will of the well-connected speculators like Livingston. Former President Martin Van Buren was made popular with the farmers when he was vice president and advising Andrew Jackson. He disliked slavery, and in 1848 he helped found and ran for president as the Free Soil Party candidate. They were against extending slavery to the new territories. He endorsed free homesteads, but his relationship with the Landlords of the Manors didn't help him, and he failed. Later when Van Buren's free-soil movement joined with the Whigs and the Anti-Rent Party the land reform movement became one of the foundations of the Republican Party. Lincoln's election made free homesteads become possible. It was the yearning by the farmers of Taconic for land reform that inspired the Homestead Act for our western lands. They demanded to be treated as equals. The dream of the farmers from this place that started just before 1750 was finally achieved when Abraham Lincoln signed the Homestead Act of 1862. An ordinary man could get a farm just by settling and working it. Political influence wasn't needed; great wealth wasn't needed; only a willingness to work and endure hardship was needed. Then he could be his own landlord.

These free farmers building their own farms with their own hands made America great. The railroad needed steel for the rails. Every house needed hinges. Every farm needed a plow. These, along with all the other things needed, paid for with wheat, corn, pigs, and the like drove the economy of the nation. It turned the nation into an industrial giant.

Back in New York the landlords didn't give up easily. There were thousands of court cases and some landlords still tried to defend their ownership and collect the rent for years. In 1848 Governor Young asked for and got legislation to recover the manors for the state unless the landlords could prove ownership. He then advocated the disposal of public land to the actual settlers. The quarter-sales reservation in the leases was ruled unconstitutional in 1850. Then on appeal it was ruled enforceable in leases written before the Revolution. Some offered the land for sale at low rates. Steven Van Rensselaer IV sold many of his leases to a speculator, Walter Church. Church pursued enforcement of many of the leases in court and won some and lost some. The last blood spilled in the movement was Deputy Sheriff Leonard Chamberlain in the early 1880s. He was serving papers for Church. Church died in 1890, virtually bankrupted. The end, however, was signaled to the Livingstons earlier. In 1852 the Court of Appeals settled the case of De Peyster *v.* Michael. De Peyster had purchased land from Van Rensselaer and sought to eject Michael for non-performance of certain manorial conditions. After Michael won, the Livingstons stopped filing new cases and retired to their mansions on the Hudson to watch the sun set in the west over the land they once owned. Further west, it was still 10 years before a new day would dawn for the homesteaders. When the Indians sold their land to the Lord of the Manor they believed that a man could only own what he could cultivate and occupy. The Indians felt they would continue to enjoy the land Livingston could not occupy. The Indians had no idea of how the manorial system worked and how Livingston could control their land by controlling the lives of others. The Livingstons had held the land for more than 150 years, but what the Indians thought was finally shown to be true. The old landlords lost their land when other men gained their rights and were free. The men who settled the land, cultivated the land, and occupied the land, owned the land.

Sources

I USED THREE PRIMARY SOURCES FOR *REBELS OF THE NORTH*.

The Documentary History of the State of New York by E.B. O'Callaghan, M.D., Albany, New York, 1850; notes taken on the Livingston Papers by Ruth Piwonka and made available by my mother Olive F. Langdon, historian of the town of Copake, NY; and *Tin Horns and Calico* by Henry Christman, Cornwallville, New York, Hope Farm Press. Henry Christman researched the trial of Dr. Boughton and the events in Delhi with the Steel murder. His book gives a fuller account of the happening concerning the trials and was an excellent source and was used extensively and quoted in places. His work differs in when the Anti-Rent War began. His book views it as starting after the death of Steven Van Rensselaer. This book views it more as a land-reform movement that started in the 1750s and was not just a protest.

Ruth's notes spurred my interest when I realized the house described in the lease was, in fact, the house I grew up in. As I looked through the *Documentary History* and discovered the Van

Deusen name I became fascinated by what was unfolding. It was a fight over land reform and against a privileged class.

The close relationship of the Copake people with the people of Mount Washington, Massachusetts, had long held my interest. My dad had been invited up to Merve Whitbeck's hunting camp many years ago to hunt deer with Babe Ruth who vacationed up there. Also, the people of the mountain shopped and got their mail in Copake Falls, New York for many years. This included families of the same last name, including Van Deusen and Whitbeck, as early settlers of Copake. What had happened in the 1750s seemed to explain why. These families fled to the mountains to be free of the Livingstons' hold.

Henry Christman's *Tin Horns and Calico* filled in where the *Documentary History* left off and included the dialog of the Copake incident. His book also covers much of the founding of the Republican Party. I had extensive family documents and artifacts to draw on. Other sources include the following:

Eighty Years' Progress of the United States, published by L. Stebbins, Hartford, CT, 1868

Columbia County at the end of the Century, The Hudson Gazette, Hudson, NY, The Record Printing & Publishing Co., 1900

The Early History of Amenia

History of Columbia County, New York, Philadelphia, PA, J. B. Lippincott & Co., 1878

Compton's Encyclopedia, 1964 Ed.

Grolier Encyclopedia, 1993

World Book Encyclopedia, 1964

Furs by Astor, John Upton, Terrell, NY, William Morrow & Company, 1963

The New York Times on Astor Library, 1974

The Mill on the Roeliff Jansen Kill, The Roeliff Jansen Historical Society Hendersonville, NY, The Black Dome Press Corp., 1993

Dutch Houses in the Hudson Valley before 1776. Helen Wilkinson, Reynolds, NY, Dover Publications, Inc., 1964

A History of Mount Washington, Mass, a dissertation, Mason Library, Great Barrington, MA, 1976

The Life and Venture of the Original John Jacob Astor, Elizabeth L. Gebhard, Bryant Printing Co., Hudson, N.Y., 1915

Scattered Leaves, Sara Nooney Hauser, Franklin, NC, Genealogy Publishing Service, 1994

Genealogical information was supplied by Ann Van Deusen, Great Barrington, MA; Peter Jensen, Copake, NY; and Eric Jensen, Chalfont, PA, who has genealogical family records holding 10,000 individual names. I also used family Bibles and Remembrances.

Index

Cromwell, Oliver, 2, 22–23
Crown, the, 4–6, 31
Crown Point, New York, 53

D
Dannamora, New York, 69
Darbie, Jonathan, 53
Decker, Abraham, 13–14
Decker, Steven, 61, 62–63
Declaration of Independence, 28, 32
Delaware County, 69
Delaware River, 47
Democratic Party, 42–43, 70–71, 76, 81
De Peyster v. Michael, 88
Devonshire, England, 16
Devyr, Thomas, 69
Dinehart, Charity Ann, 15–16
Dinehart, Elizabeth Snyder, 15–16
Dinehart, John, 15–16
Dinehart, Malvina, 15
Dinehart, William, 13–14
Dinehart Farm, 14
Donation Land Act, 74
Dorr, Russell, 67–68
Douglas, Stephen, 76, 80–82
Dred Scott Decision, 79
Duke of York, 1, 2
Durham, Connecticut, 72
Dutch, 5, 8, 10, 13, 21, 22, 25, 31, 47–48
Dutchess County, 12, 16
Dutch West India Company, 8

E
Earle, Moses, 69
East India Company, 4, 30
Elkhart, Indiana, 18
Endicott, John, 22
England, 12, 22

English Civil War, 2
English Manor system, 20
English Revolution, 22
Erie Canal, 13, 18
Europe, 25
Evertt, Edward, 82

F
Fallen Timbers, Battle of, 40
Federalist Constitution of 1777, 71
Federalist Party, 27, 33, 56, 70
Federal Mint, 46
Feudal law, 20, 25–29, 38, 55, 71, 75, 83–84, 87
Fillmore, Millard, 76, 78
Finkle, George L., 57, 61, 65
Finkle, Peter, 47, 57, 61
Florida, 41
Fort Stanwix, 12
Franklin, Benjamin, 31, 32, 69
Freedom of the press, 6
Free Soil Party, 70, 75–76, 87
Fremont, John, 78–79
French and Indian War, 12, 25, 31, 53
French Revolution, 28–29
Fulton, Robert, 33, 41
Furlong, Matthew, 53

G
Gage, General, 17
Gardiner Manor, Lord of, 4
Gardiners Island, 4, 5
George, King, 18
George, Lloyd, 27
George III, King, 34
Georgia, 16, 21, 37, 43, 75, 82
German Palatines, 5
Glorious Revolution, 2
Grant, Jesse, 39
Grant, U.S., 39